LOST & FOUND

Finding *Success* in the Search for Self

LOST & FOUND
Finding *Success* in the Search for Self

JACARI HARRIS

CONTENTS

APPENDICES

Every day that we wake up and step outside or just take a breath, we hope that our mistakes don't follow us around now that we know better. Someday, we'll get the chance to be everything that we hope that we are, now that we look in the mirror.

– Jacari Harris

This book is dedicated to those who continue to overcome life's obstacles, and to those who are being strong and courageous, hoping to believe that they too can achieve success.

Author's Note

This is a true account based on my memory and recollections, although some details of my story occurred before I was conceived or immediately after I began walking. I have done my best to confirm the facts. Some names have been changed to protect the privacy of individuals.

FOREWORD

Benjamin L. Crump, Esq.

I met Jacari Harris on May 30, 2014, about one year after the State of Florida v. George Zimmerman trial for the shooting of Trayvon Martin, a seventeen-year-old who was walking the streets of The Retreat at Twin Lakes in Sanford, Florida with only a bag of Skittles and a bottle of iced tea. As one of the leading attorneys on the case, I was able to witness millions of young people across our world stand up for what they believe in. One of those "young people" was Jacari. My passion for advocacy has given me the privilege to fight for justice on behalf of the marginalized in our country, a calling to which I'm dedicated to. Jacari's advocacy efforts for foster youth and adopted individuals is touching the lives of many of those who are affected by foster care or adoption, policy makers, businesses, and people who didn't know anything about either of the two.

When Jacari first entered the law firm, I was in my office preparing for some interviews with clients that were scheduled for the top of the hour. Since the Trayvon case, we had been backed up from other clients and started receiving more requests to represent families all over the country. We had no time to waste, so when Jacari stepped foot in the doors of the law firm, the entire staff was concerned that we'd not get the days' worth of work completed if we stopped to service him. When my receptionist came to the back to speak to Adner (my communications director) and I about a teenager seeking employment, we both laughed, because no one stops by unless they have a pre-arranged meeting that was most likely scheduled weeks in advance, and we weren't hiring anymore people. With no prior arrangements, I informed my receptionist to give him a business card that had the general office email—the email account that many constituents use when they're wanting our services or just have general inquiries. It was the expectation that he'd take it and leave, so someone could get back with him later, and that we could continue working. He took the card from her then requested that he still speak or introduce himself to someone in the office before he left. After the receptionist came back and reported this information, I went ahead and informed Adner to talk to him. I didn't know what they'd talk about, because we had no information on him; however, even though he had no business coming on our grounds, he made it his business to leave with what he asked for: an opportunity to learn and grow. As the eighteen-year-old shared his high school journey and post-graduate plans, I knew that he was the man with a plan. His determination led me to sign off on a full-time internship with the law firm that would start the next business day. I was hesitant to sign-off at first because our application and acceptance rate is very rigorous, and we usually only accept law school students or graduate students. But because he was a black, teenage male like Trayvon was, I wanted to take him in and groom him for future generations.

I left the office thinking two things:

1. I need to invest as much as I can in him while I have his attention; and
2. He could be another Trayvon Martin.

Within the first week, he was already like family to everyone in the firm, and he completed his tasks exceedingly well. I learned more about him and where his braveness, determination, and willingness to impact others triggered from—his own story. Without him having to tell me much, I could see it in his walk and how he conducted himself throughout the trip to Atlanta, Georgia when I was a candidate for the National Bar Association's (NBA) General President position. Though he was the only intern that came with us from the office, and one of the youngest volunteers throughout the entire conference, his hard work did not go unnoticed. In fact, quite a few of my colleagues asked me about him, and how was I able to get him to intern for my office. Many of them couldn't believe the story of how his internship came about, but one thing they knew for sure was that he was going places further than he could believe with his work ethic, and dedication to achieving his goals.

Like everyone who knows Jacari's story of being in foster care and adopted, I'm inspired by his determination. I also appreciate his transparency. Adoption is a vital subject that isn't spoken about enough. With the hundreds of thousands of youth in our world's foster care system, we need more families to get involved to help ensure that all youth have a place to call "home." As the guardian of two adopted cousins, Marcus and Chancellor, I know firsthand how adoption can impact the lives of vulnerable youth.

As Jacari is my mentee, I am looking forward to seeing the many things that he will accomplish in his life, even after releasing his first book. I have no idea what he will do or how he will continue to impact the masses; but one thing I do know for sure is that he will get it done, no matter what it takes.

This is just the beginning. Who knows what else he's up to? Look at how far he's come! Who are we to decide his next steps? He's walking in his purpose, and I'll be there every step of the way to cheer him on!

Through a steadfast dedication to justice and service, renowned civil rights and personal injury attorney

Benjamin Crump has established himself as one of the nation's foremost lawyers and advocates for social justice. He has worked on some of the most high-profile cases in the U.S., representing the families of George Floyd, Trayvon Martin, Michael Brown, Stephon Clark, as well as the residents of Flint, Michigan, who were affected by the poisoned water of the Flint River. He has been nationally recognized as the 2014 NNPA Newsmaker of the Year, The National Trial Lawyers Top 100 Lawyers, and Ebony Magazine Power 100 Most Influential African Americans. In 2016, he was designated as an Honorary Fellow by the University of Pennsylvania College of Law. His book, published in October 2019, *Open Season: Legalized Genocide of Colored People,* reflects on the landmark cases he has battled, and how discrimination in the courthouse devastates real families and communities. He is married to Dr. Genae Angelique Crump, is the proud father of Brooklyn Zeta Crump, and the guardian of two adopted cousins, Marcus and Chancellor. He is the founder and principal owner of Ben Crump Law.

PREFACE

Getting Lost

I didn't know any better once I moved to the other side of the tracks. I couldn't hear the music from the snow-cone man's truck coming miles away anymore. I couldn't see the children nearby run to the black metal gate and put their hands through the hole to give up their last coins for a red or blue snow-cone that would melt in seconds. Those days were far gone. I wasn't living with the woman who carried me for nine months anymore. I didn't have to worry about hiding under the bed or in the closet when the police department would randomly come to the apartment because they knew my mother had a drug history. I lived somewhere else now.

Peanut (whose real name is Telvin), my older brother who came with me during the separation was popping his lips because he wanted his way. Clothes and shoes were getting tossed inside of black garbage bags by the people who came to take us away. We were just sitting there with droopy faces, crying because we didn't have a clue as to what was really going on. We'd seen our mother getting arrested and heard her wailing, crying. I remember sitting in the backseat of a mini-van, looking at all the trees that we'd passed by on the road—headed to a destination that I thought, and hoped, would be our everlasting home. We ended up staying there for days, weeks, and those weeks turned into months until we were put up for adoption. Peanut would continue to pop his lips and make a weird noise with his tongue. Almost like a sigh, but it would last longer. It's my belief that he wanted anyone and everyone to listen to what he had to say—but he rarely talked. That's because many people didn't really know him; if they did, they would know that he held everything in.

I knew I was different when I was sitting on the floor looking in the mirror wondering why my nose was flatter and my ears were smaller than the people that lived in the other rooms in the house that I would soon call "home." The woman who took us in didn't remind me of my biological mother—maybe because majority of the time my biological mother was on drugs, so I was not accustomed to a mother-figure who was calm and welcoming. Her son was staying there at the time. In fact, he's still there to this day. We look nothing alike. "Brothers" with no features in common.

Days after the move, I heard stories of how other people's children had slept in the same room that was now mine. I saw pictures of children smiling and looking happy.

Mama (the woman who took us in) shared different stories with us about her former foster children. She believed that all a child needed was to be and feel loved and disciplined, so, as she would say, "They can grow up to be somebody. As the two-year-old that I was, I really didn't care about what was being said nor could I really comprehend what was going on; however, after getting to know Mama, I realized she wanted us to "grow up to be somebody" because she'd invested so much in us, and she wanted to make sure that we were ready for what the world had to offer to each of us.

The household was full of stories from the people who came before me, but the people who no longer lived in the house did not share their story as Mama did. She explained by saying that her previous foster children did not want to share because they were scared that someone would judge them, even though her home was a safe space for all stories.

I have come to realize that every human on this Earth will be judged no matter what the situation is. And it is time now to release those untold stories that have kept us all up at night, and help our fellow brothers and sisters get through life by the lessons learned in our own lives.

We all have an untold story, whether it is about overcoming an obstacle, renewal or rebirth, a quest, journey and return, tragedy, or even a comedy. Whatever it may be, it changed us in a way that we never saw coming; good or bad, different or indifferent, it's our story. Never change the originality of it, but instead, accept what has occurred. Appreciate it and grow from it.

Adoption is a story within itself. How it originated, when it originated, what country it started in, how effective it has been over time, and the lives that have changed from it—whether it be the adoptee, adopter, or the birth parents.

Life is not set up to be a fairytale. It was never written that it would be easy nor was it ever stated that pain and grief would always last.

As I write this story, I encourage you to release, let go, and be the person you are destined to be, though you may be dismayed, confused, or even worried; this day, time, and place have been created just for you. My story is just that—my story. As I wrote every word in this book, it is not my goal to down or ridicule anyone or anything. No one is perfect, but everyone has a perfect story to tell to help someone else. I simply went back in time to understand who I really am, and what really happened to me before, during and after I was placed in foster care. I had to do this or my purpose in life wouldn't be fulfilled.

I didn't give up on myself despite all the difficulties that I went through. You have the power to control your future. Stay true to yourself. Never underestimate your ability to achieve the things that your heart yearns for.

Where you are today will benefit you tomorrow.

For I was chosen. I was wanted. I was cherished. I grew in their hearts. I was the missing piece. I was loved. I was… adopted.

THE REASONING BEHIND IT ALL

I could barely walk when I was taken from my parents. I was dropped off at a friend of the family by the lady who birthed me and was later picked up by The Department of Children and Families, with no real explanation.

My mother had a long history of crack and alcohol abuse, one of millions in the U.S. in the 1990s. On October 21, 1997, a shelter hearing was held, and my brother and I were placed in shelter care. It was proven that our mother had left us with a family friend, Nikki. Nikki was informed by our mother that she would return in an hour; however, she did not return for three days. Nikki was a full-time employee who had called out to work two of the three days we were with her, hoping that our mother would return. But after countless un-answered phone calls, and after getting advice from other neighbors, she felt she had no choice but to get others involved. Some of my siblings were much older than I was, I'm sure they could have looked after us when Nikki could not. I also can't blame Nikki's for contacting others to help us out, because she knew something wasn't right. According to the police report, we were left in a dirty, unkempt condition with no provisions for our care such as diapers and clean clothing. Anytime someone is babysitting children, the parent must ensure the sitter has all the necessary essentials for the kids. During the three days my mother was gone, she was seen walking the streets. Witnesses stated she appeared drunk or high on crack, unbalanced with slurred speech, an angry disposition, and wearing the same clothes for days. Though this information was presented to a judge, I would like to know what really happened to our mother during the three days. I saw no sign of her being drunk or high before she left. Who did she go with? Where did she go? Why didn't the people who picked her up bring her back? The more I thought about it growing up, the more questions I had, but it was too late to ask those questions. She'd already gotten caught up in that web of destructive behavior and in the criminal system.

7. NEED FOR PLACEMENT - Placement of the child(ren) in shelter care is in the best interest of the child(ren); continuation in the home is contrary to the welfare of the child(ren) because the home situation presents a substantial and immediate danger which cannot be mitigated by the provision of preventive services and placement is necessary to protect the child(ren) as shown by the following facts:

X the child(ren) was/were abused, abandoned, or neglected, or is/are suffering from or in imminent danger of injury or illness as a result of abuse, abandonment, or neglect, specifically: This mother left her children with a family friend on Thursday October 16 and promised to return on Friday October 17. The children were left with no provisions and the mother did not return as agreed. The children were transported to a family members home. However, this mother and a companion came to the family members home and took the children away. Both the mother and her companion were alleged to be intoxicated. Also, this mother's IPS counselor has continually encouraged mother to attend FASC, but to no avail.

___ the custodian has materially violated a condition of placement imposed by the court, specifically:

OR

___ the child(ren) has/have no parent, legal custodian, or responsible adult relative immediately known and available to provide supervision and care, specifically:

OR

Judicial Review Social Study Report/Case Plan Update/Permanency Review, FL. Circuit Court, 2nd Judicial Court § 39.453(6)(a), Florida Statutes (1999).

3

As a child, though, among the many questions I had, the ones that hurt the most was wondering whether our mother forgot about us, the children she left. Did she forget about the long, tight hugs we would give her in the mornings or at night? Or our big, smiling faces? I've looked for, but can't seem to find, the answers to these questions. The police report doesn't answer any them, and I'm sure that my mother wouldn't remember a second of the day back then. She was drunk and on drugs—all she could remember was the feeling. If anything, she wished that she could erase that day and never think of it again, because the day the police came was the day all hell broke loose.

For months, we were minors under the jurisdiction of the court of Leon County, Florida, out of touch with our biological parents and siblings. Peanut and I were the only of my siblings paired together in a foster home. A case plan was put into effect by the judge and agency on the third day of April 1998 as an attempt for all my brothers and sisters to be able to go back with our biological family.

At the time, I was almost two years old— youngest of seven— Peanut was four, and my eldest sister was twenty-two and pregnant. We really didn't know what was going on at such a young age, and the court had jurisdiction over our wellbeing until the case concluded and a decision was made in our best interest. Eventually, we had the case plan that was consistent with similar cases and that upheld all necessary requirements.

We were to be placed in a setting which was as family-like and as close to the original home as possible, with the children's best interests and special needs in mind. The closest location to our original home that they could get us placed was about thirty minutes away. At that time, according to the Florida court system, our return to our mother's custody would be contrary to the best interest and welfare of us, her children.

1. BACKGROUND

    A. Date of Removal: **Oct. 20, 1997**

    B. Date of Disposition into Substitute Care: **April 20, 1998**

    C. Total Months in Care as of this Review: **22 months - Telvin & Jacari (October 21, 1997) 17 months - Kayla & Shalonda (March 11, 1998)**

    D. Reason for Protective Services / Placement In Substitute Care: **These children had previously been adjudicated dependent on August 29, 1989. The children were placed in shelter on October 21, 1997 by order of the Court due to abandonment & neglect because of mother's substance abuse.**

Judicial Review Social Study Report/Case Plan Update/Permanency Review, FL. Circuit Court, 2nd Judicial Court § 39.453(6)(a), Florida Statutes (1999).

My biological mother's name was Fanny. She had five baby daddies. My father, Edward, had more children with more different women than one can count on two hands. To date, he has nineteen children. The family court in charge of our case sought for him to build a stronger relationship with my sisters, brother, and me, to provide emotionally and physically for us. Both parents were ordered to complete parenting classes, but they never showed up. My mother was in and out of the system, starting and stopping the work she needed to do on her case plan to get us. My father's priorities weren't aligned with his children's.

My mother's case plan had an end goal of getting all her children back to her by September 21, 1998. The court ordered our mother to complete a substance abuse program once more—she had completed the same program years prior for her substance abuse issues. This time, she couldn't miss more than one session, she had to follow all recommendations by the therapists, and she needed to provide the agency with documentation upon completion of sessions. She'd then have to remain drug free and comply with random urinalysis when requested by the counselor or the department and provide that documentation upon completion. In addition, she had to secure and maintain employment while having cold and hot running water, a functioning bathroom and kitchen facilities, and adequate bed space for all her children in a space free of all health and safety hazards. People make their own decisions. However, when faced with so much turmoil, and no one, including family, to help steer you in the right direction, you have a greater possibility of failing within the system. In this case, my mother had failed within the system. She didn't receive as much help as she needed. The foster care agency that managed our case and court issuing her case plan knew that she didn't have a car or money. So how was she supposed to get to and from the parenting sessions? She couldn't work a standard nine-to-five job, because the counseling sessions assigned would have interfered with her work schedule at Wendy's. I am not putting the blame for her actions or this situation on the agency or state- because she ultimately didn't comply. But realistically, no one can be at two different places at one time.

Over the years, I have met parents who've had their children taken away from them. Some days, they had to choose between going to sessions and going to work. Some people may not see an issue in doing that; however, these same parents who tried their best to get their children back gave up and reverted to drinking and doing drugs (as my mother did) because the process was so overwhelming for them. Not to mention, they were viewed as horrible individuals when they meant good; they just needed effective resources that would allow balance between work, life, and their case plan.

Fanny's attorney decided to close the case due to her non-compliance. She was involved in treatment at a recovery facility that would provide services for her based upon her individual needs as assessed through comprehensive evaluations during the in-take process and throughout her participation in the program. Due to her disruptive and disrespectful behavior toward fellow clients, she was asked to leave. She wasn't attending the substance abuse treatment program, either.

According to her attorney, she continued to provide excuses as to why she hadn't attended sessions on a regular basis such as transportation problems, lack of money, sickness, the difficulties of moving to another apartment since she wasn't getting along with her neighbors.

By December of 1998, all seven of her children had been placed outside of her residence. Four out of seven of us went to foster homes, my older brother stayed with a relative of the family, and my oldest sister was considered a legal adult. She moved out to get her own apartment. A petition for termination of parental rights for all the minor children was filed with the court on December 2, 1998. The only two people who really knew what was taking place were my eldest brother and sister, who were old enough to comprehend what had happened to our family. But even they couldn't piece everything together, because they didn't want to see our mother in the predicament that she was in.

On July 5, 1999, the termination of her parental rights was complete.

The substance abuse that my biological mother endured caused her to be incapable of caring for my siblings and myself. Efforts to explore relatives and locate temporary or permanent placement weren't successful. There were no other relatives who were able or willing to care for four out of six of us. Instead, the four of us would stay with the foster parents that took us in. My other two siblings were taken in by a relative. We'd then have to attend counseling and seek behavior specialists to cope with the reality of our circumstances under the direction of our counselor.

Instead of moving around to other foster homes, the case manager created a permeant placement plan that would have to be achieved by our foster parents to be adopted. Once the placement plan was executed and bi-weekly status reports from the case manager deemed that I was happy in the foster home; my foster mother started completing a home study to be licensed to adopt, which was soon-after achieved.

THE AWAKENING

B y the time I was elementary age, we'd long since started calling our foster mother "Mama." My brother and I learned many things with her: cooking, baking, cleaning, washing clothes, showing good manners, and valuing church attendance. Having bad manners was Mama's biggest pet peeve. Teaching us how to say please and thank you, ensuring that we knew the proper way to speak to someone, to open doors for women, and help the elderly were very important to her. Her biological son, Aymin, lived with us as well. He had his own bedroom, and there were two more bedrooms that she'd open to her foster children. At the time, she was only fostering Peanut and me, after her last foster youth had been reunited with their biological parents. So, we had our own rooms—but it was often temporary because Mama could get a phone call from the Department of Children and Families anytime of the day asking her to taken in more children.

My ultimate favorite thing Mama taught me was cooking. Any time that I would see her go into the kitchen, I made it a priority to assist her. She was so happy in the kitchen, as if it was her favorite room in the house. Her smile would get bigger as she was preparing food. I could tell that she loved feeding people. And it wasn't microwavable food either. It was always slow-cooked, oven roasted, deep fried, or steamed food accompanied by freshly baked breads. Most times, I could tell exactly what she was going to cook, because she left out the meat and other ingredients on the counter in the morning. I knew she was very serious about her cooking when she'd take down all the seasonings, she planned on using and placed them with the ingredients for dinner. This way she could get to them easily, and she would know what she needed to pick up from the store on her way home from work. When she'd cook, I could smell the onions and bell peppers that she'd pre-cut with her cutting knife. Or, if she wasn't in the mood to cut up her own vegetables, she would get me to do it for her. She would always find a way to use her onions and green peppers. She believed they belonged in everything and helped to bring out the taste in food.

I will never forget the broken wood cabinets with cobwebs in the corners in the kitchen where she made her meals. Although the paint was slowly coming off them, they still held up. My favorite cabinet was the one that had the most damage. The knob was barely hanging on and the two remaining shelves weren't stable. The bottom shelf had Kool-Aid stains from packs of Kool-Aid ripped open by Peanut or me. We'd sometimes be thirsty, and we knew that we could only drink water until it was time for dinner, yet we'd sneak the Kool-Aid packages, get a drinking cup, fill it with water and insert the entire package in the cup, mixing both the water and Kool-Aid together. Then we'd pour Mama's sugar, which was strictly for her coffee, directly into the cup so she wouldn't hear us. If we had leftover juice, we'd hide it in the closet in our room for later.

That cabinet was jam-packed with junk food. Mama let us go to Wal-Mart with her, where she shopped for a month's worth of groceries at a time. She would buy food stamps from relatives. Mama would call her cousin Shirley, who had six children, because she knew that she would have food stamps. Peanut and I would overhear her on the phone begging for food stamps. She'd ask, "Do you have any extra food stamps that I can buy? The boys eat like grown men."

Mama knew the answer would be "yes," because she'd never call anyone who didn't have many children. The more children someone had, the more food stamps they'd receive. And if Shirley couldn't come through with food stamps for the month, Mama had a backup. Mama would then go on to say, "Well, how much food stamps do you have?" She sounded desperate when she asked, but she never qualified for food stamps when she applied. Her high school diploma, job as a receptionist for the state, and voluntary dependents through fostering—receiving less than four hundred dollars a month per child to do so—the government felt she had more than enough to get by.

I couldn't understand why Mama continued asking those people for food stamps knowing she didn't qualify. She bought food stamps from family and friends for half on the dollar. In return, they got cash to buy or pay for things that couldn't be bought with food stamps. This is a common practice among poor people, but I didn't think we were poor. I just thought she was always trying to get good deals. She'd never tell us if her money was low; she always found a way to make us happy. We didn't see the blood, sweat, and tears she kept behind closed doors, because she didn't want us to know that she was struggling sometimes too.

Although now as an adult who's qualified for food stamps, I don't agree with what Mama did. Purchasing food stamps is illegal. And I feel as if the person who provided the card to Mama would be losing out on money, and food they might need in the future. Especially since the purpose of the federally funded program is to assist low-income families with food to meet their dietary needs.

Every time Mama carried us to the store with her, she would try to make one of us push the cart and the other pick up items as she walked beside us. She spoke to everyone she knew, or at least, thought she knew. When we would get on her nerves from asking her to buy a toy or snacks, she'd let us walk around the store while she finished shopping Before we left her sight, she'd give us the lecture: "Don't touch anything unless you can pay for it." Not to mention, if we stole something, we would go to jail. She was always sure to throw that one in. We'd nod our heads and go about our way—touching everything in sight, even if we didn't want it.

Mama went to the same grocery stores—Harvey's or Piggly Wiggly for most of the groceries and Publix for bread and fruit—so we knew the stores well. Every time we'd watch TV, you could count on Peanut or me having a notepad and pencil by us. We'd create a list of snacks we wanted to get at the grocery store. I'd try to be healthy and list fruits and peanuts; Peanut ask for mostly Little Debbie snacks and candy. If Mama agreed to buy these, we'd usually share. That's unless we were mad at each other, which never lasted long: we were all we had.

When we finished getting our snacks at the store, we would grab Mama's, too. Peanut would suck his teeth, aggravated, because he thought we were wasting time. He didn't think it made sense since she could get them herself. I thought it made perfect sense because she would be glad that we'd thought about her. I knew she would complain that we were being selfish, or that we never thought about her while we were getting our snacks. To better convince her to buy what we wanted, we had to get her something as well.

At check-out, Mama was very particular about how she wanted her items bagged. Chicken could only be bagged with chicken; cold foods could not be in the same bag as dry foods. She wanted her bread in a separate bag, eggs in a bag to themselves, cans together, et cetera. This made it easier to put up the groceries once we got home. Mama did her best to find coupons so she could save money. Mama would hide some of the groceries from us at home, so we wouldn't eat them all. She didn't believe in wasting food or eating just because it was available.

Some nights, I had trouble sleeping and would wake up in the middle of the night and wander around the house. I'd always go to Peanut's room first, but he was usually asleep. Then, I'd go to Mama's bedroom; she would be snoring. Sometimes she would wake up when I walked in her room and tell me to get in her bed. Sometimes we'd talk about things that'd happened in the past. The times she didn't wake up, I wondered if she just didn't want to talk. After leaving her room, I'd peek in on my foster-siblings, if Mama had any at the time. When she did have more children to foster, they most likely would be asleep. Then, I would go in the kitchen for a snack.

I remember being terrified to get caught sneaking snacks, especially if I didn't finish my dinner the night before. I always heard Mama say, "You better eat that food because somebody's child wasn't able to eat tonight," as if I was accustomed to eating dinner every night before coming to Mama. Deep inside, I was thankful. Thankful because she didn't have to take my brother or I in, but she did.

Mama would always demand that her house be clean before she got home. She believed that since she went to work and paid the bills, we should do the housework work. I didn't mind doing this, because I loved to clean. Plus, Mama deserved a break when she got home. We lived in a four-bedroom, two-bathroom mobile home surrounded by trees and other mobile homes. It didn't look like a mobile home, because Mama got the vinyl siding replaced with red bricks. When her daughter, Vickie, passed away due to a heart attack, Mama had a portion of Vickie's mobile home connected to her house, so she could have a den and an extra bedroom. It was an overall large home, with walk-in closets and a big kitchen. Mama never liked her home, because she knew that it was constructed with cheap material. Something would always break, or a leak would occur that she had to get fixed immediately, or else her water bill would be high. Some of the walls would suddenly get swollen, and in her room, brownish liquid would stream down the wall and stain it. Though the trailer wasn't in the best condition, I always found a way to make it look nice and smell clean. First, I'd write a checklist of what needed to be done, for it was critical that I completed all cleaning tasks.

When it was time for Mama to arrive home from work, I'd sit patiently on the living room floor, waiting for her arrival. Peanut was usually at a friend's house when Mama got home. As soon as I saw her gold Kia Sedona minivan's reflection in the living room window, I'd run outside barefoot so I could help her bring whatever she had purchased inside the house. Mama always looked drained from the workday. She was short, round-faced, and wore velvet lipstick. Her hair was usually done. If she didn't have a sew-in, she would wear one of the three wigs she owned. As she settled in, I'd tell her all about the cleaning Peanut and I had done—mostly me. Peanut would stop and play video games or would still be cleaning his room. After she was done inspecting our work, she would lay in her bed and watch the news or a cooking show.

THE UNWANTED VISITS

I often wondered what the members of my biological family were doing. They didn't bother to check on Peanut or me, Or, maybe, they didn't know how to get in contact with us. There were so many moving components during the separation. Looking back now, everyone was overwhelmed and wanted to move on with their own lives. I tried not to think on that too much. I knew if we hadn't heard from our biological mother, she was most likely behind bars. "For what now?" I would often ask myself. Maybe my biological mother thought I didn't need to know her faults since I was already taken away. Or, maybe she didn't want me to know about her struggles with alcohol and drug addiction. Now that years had gone by, I believed I was wise enough to comprehend her faults and help her get on the right track, or so I thought.

I thought my biological mother would get tired of going through the same cycle court, jail, and foster care agencies. I concluded incorrectly because, though she wished for things to get back right, her priorities weren't in order. The very few times that she was doing better and not drinking or on any drugs, she'd call Peanut and me on Mama's phone during her time allotted her by the state. Most of the time, she'd cry out to us, telling Peanut and I that she wasn't going to drink or do drugs anymore and how she'd given her life to God, so she was now a "changed woman." I'd put the phone on mute, and Peanut and I would giggle, because we heard the same story all those other times that she'd called too. Her crying was a cry for help, but we couldn't do much more than encourage her to do right. By that time, Peanut and I were back to sharing a room with a bunk bed, and any night we would get off the phone with our biological mother, I could hear the bed rails squeaking from Peanut tossing and turning periodically. I figured he was having nightmares; especially after hearing our mother on the phone squealing. I'd be afraid to go back to sleep, because I didn't want to have a nightmare—we were already living in one. Just him and me, in a dark, cold world, separated from the ones that were supposed to make us feel whole again. We were surrounded by love from our new family, but that didn't mean much because we wanted the love and attention from our real parents.

Even if we couldn't stay with our mother, our father also wasn't there. At times, I wondered if he would step up, or if I would ever have a father figure in my life. He was already a statistic, a dead-beat father. I couldn't help but be a statistic as well, even if I didn't want to. It was no fault of my own, but as soon as I was placed in the system, the mark was made.

In addition to the calls with biological mother, the judge set up visitation with our parents—again, during the times that our mother was doing better. These visitations started when I was three years old. At that time, we had bi-weekly Friday supervised visits at McDonald's for one hour. We rarely had them because my mother was in and out of jail and our father never showed up. Plus, it was hard to meet at a certain time because my other siblings were placed with different families.

The few times we did meet, the transporter noted how happy we were and how well we interacted with our mom. Our time always seemed to go too quickly, especially when our mother showed up. When we parted ways, our mother would always start to cry, which caused us to become upset and cry as well. Our transporter would remind Peanut and I that we would have more opportunities to see our mother and other siblings—but that didn't resolve our fears, our sadness, our anxieties. She had to drive us away and carry us back to our foster homes.

Not knowing when I'd see my family again was difficult. I was three years old at the first visitation, and I was going with the flow. However, as I grew older and was under Mama's legal guardianship., she continued to allow us to visit with our mother on a bi-weekly basis. I couldn't understand how a judge could think one hour was enough time with our parents and siblings. We all needed attention, we all wanted to be loved on, and an hour just wasn't enough. As much as I wanted to speak out, I didn't because I was a minor; in their eyes, I didn't know much.

After visits the transporter would drop us off at Mama's job, which was a tall state building off Suwannee Street. From there we would wait for her to get off work I loved it, because Peanut and I would sit in the cafeteria and have leftovers from lunch, or her coworkers would bring us treats. Mama would brag about us to her co-workers and tell them when we would be in the building, because they loved us just as much as she did. If we didn't go to her job, we'd get picked up by Mama's sister (our next-door neighbor) who would drive home, so we could clean up the house.

One night, as I was in the den drawing on my notepad, I heard four hard knocks on our front door. It sounded as if the police were trying to break down our door. I then remembered that Mama mentioned she was expecting a visitor, but after weeks went by with no visitor coming by, I didn't expect anyone to show up. I was nervous, so I walked swiftly to my room, trying not to make much noise, because Mama didn't like people running in the house. If she caught someone running, she'd make you go back and walk. When I made it to my room, I got in the bed and hid under my pillows and sheets to pretend as if I was asleep. That way, I wouldn't have to be the person to open the door.

By the time I was able to shut my eyes tight, Mama called for me from the other side of the house. Her tone was pleasant, so I knew I wasn't in trouble, but I couldn't figure out what she wanted. Peanut didn't make it any better. I heard his door closing. Bullets of sweat came running down my forehead. I didn't know what I was walking into. I reached for my emergency bag—the bag that had one outfit, a few pairs of underwear, and small personal items—just in case they were here to take us away.

When I got to the door, the visitor seemed calm, was dressed nicely, and had freckles and curly hair. Mama told her she could have a seat, which automatically prompted me to ask the lady if she wanted anything to drink. We were taught how to treat guests of the house and that they should always be offered something. I gave her two options: too-sweet Kool-Aid, my favorite, or faucet water with ice cubes. She asked me what type of Kool-Aid it was, and, honestly, I didn't know how to describe it because I mixed the flavors. She went ahead and chose the second option, which seemed right down her alley.

Returning to the living room with her drink, I saw that the woman had gotten comfortable in my favorite seat in the living room, with her briefcase on the floor to the right of her. It was the burgundy recliner seat that Mama didn't like people sitting on, unless they were going to use it for its main purpose (to recline). She smiled. *What does she want from me?* I wondered. *Why is she staring at me as if I have done her wrong?* As I handed her the water, my mind raced with the reasons for her visit. Eventually, she said, "I am your caseworker."

Caseworker? I thought. The look on my face gave away how I really felt. Mama cleared her throat as a sign to get my act together. I didn't know the meaning of "caseworker" until I looked it up in the dictionary. Moments later, questions were being asked of me as if I knew the answer to all of them.

1. How are you feeling?
2. Have you been eating?

3. Do you like your new home?
4. Are you happy with how everything is going?
5. Do you want/need anything?
6. When was the last time you saw your brothers or sisters?

I answered each question to the best of my ability. As a young child in that position, I didn't think it was right for me to be asked, "Are you happy with how everything is going?" as if I was just supposed to be happy with being taken away from my biological mother. It wasn't my fault that any of this was happening.

After a while, the caseworker decided to leave me alone, realizing that I was not in the mood to speak about the topic. I walked swiftly to the bathroom, drowning in my own tears. Was it because I didn't like being questioned, or was it because I really didn't understand what was happening? I stayed in the bathroom, hoping the caseworker would leave, but Mama and the woman were making small talk. Mama even told her about the seven-up pound cake in the kitchen. Mama knew we didn't share homemade cakes with just anyone, so it felt like a violation for her to even discuss it. Finally, I heard the caseworker leave, signaling that the visit was over.

Now, I figured I could go back to my normal self. Only, about an hour after the visit, I was called to the kitchen. I wished Mama would have just yelled what she needed, rather than have me get up and come to her. After she continually called my name, I got up and sat at the counter, getting questioned as to why I didn't speak up and answer the caseworker's questions. Not only that, I was getting talked to as if I had been disrespectful to the freckle-faced lady. I knew that if I replied, Mama would have seen that as rude, so I just sat and listened. I knew why she wanted me to answer the questions. The caseworker was assessing Mama on her ability to abide by our case plan, which required that she provide adequate care, supervision, and daily needs of food, clothing, shelter, and medical care. Of course, she most certainly was; I just didn't want to talk to the caseworker about it.

Mama finally allowed me to leave, so I went back to my room and played with my Yo-Yo and car wheelers. Peanut still had not gotten home from the neighbors', so I had no one to play with. As soon as I began to relax, I heard another knock at the front door. I nearly peed in my clothes this time. I couldn't take someone else questioning me. Seconds later, I heard a shout. "Jacari, get up and check the door!"

This time, it was a tall, broad man. He looked as if he was in a work uniform, navy blue slacks and a white collared buttoned-down shirt with some form of logo on the left breast. After staring for what felt like hours, I eventually invited him into the house. I knew he wasn't a typical visitor, and I didn't want to go through what I had experienced with the caseworker earlier that evening. After he stepped inside, he said he was an inspector. I hadn't signed up for an inspection, and I didn't think Mama had signed up for one, either. This was our house; Mama had paid all the bills, so there was no reason for anyone to inspect anything within its walls. At least, that's what I thought.

Minutes later, after the man pulled out his clipboard and laptop, and Mama finally walked out and greeted him. Not many words passed between them; he got straight to what he came to do. The clipboard had several sheets of paper and a pad that was torn. He was struggling to keep the sheets in order, so he separated them one by one and wrote numbers in chronological order with a Sharpie at the top right of the pages.

As he started roaming the house, he opened and closed doors multiple times, pressed against the walls, checked the refrigerator and freezer temperatures. Mama followed him like she was about to get in trouble. The inspector looked for the fire extinguisher and played with it before he realized that he didn't know how to work it. Then, he went outside with Mama following along, looking at the backyard and around the house.

Moments later, the inspector and my mama came back in the house, the inspector suggesting she get the floors fixed and hire a lawn company to cut the branches on the trees hanging over the house. Looking back, Mama was a single mother with a fixed income; she did her best always, even when it looked rough. We were content, and that was the only thing that mattered. A few minutes later, the inspector told her she'd passed the inspection. I hadn't seen such a smile on Mama in weeks.

Afterward, the inspector began packing up his items to leave and go next door. As he left, he yelled, "Bye, Jessie! Bye, Jacari." My eyes opened wide, curious to know how he knew my name. Of course, I didn't ask, because I felt it was a rude question, so I just continued to go with the flow. When the door finally closed, I shut my eyes tightly, then opened them as a release.

Peanut finally came home. He was sweaty and dirty, "smelling like the outside," as Mama would say. He'd been gone most of the day, but he knew he had to get home before the porch light turned on—the difference between living in the country versus living in the city. In the city, the streetlights were the signal for when we needed to be in the house, but in the country, we had to wait for the porch light, which didn't have an automatic sensor. Mama would turn it on when she felt it should be on, typically right when the sun started setting.

Mama then called us into the kitchen to eat dinner. It was my favorite meal of all time: fried catfish nuggets, baked beans, and fries. Mama would always fry the fish a little extra hard and jazz up her baked beans the way Peanut and I liked them. She would put mustard, sugar, cinnamon, honey, and syrup in them. No one in the neighborhood could touch my mama's cooking. Before we were almost done eating, Mama handed us a bowl of fresh mixed salad. She always said it was good to have some type of veggies during a meal so that we could stay healthy and be her strong young men one day. Some evenings, she'd pile more veggies on our plates than anything. Peanut would eat everything except the veggies then cry until Mama told him to take a shower and go to bed for not eating all his food. Before all of that, she'd give a lecture on how many people wished they could eat, but didn't have the opportunity, which was why I always tried to be thankful.

When it came to me eating my vegetables, I wouldn't eat them as much, if at all but I wouldn't cry. I'd reach for something on the table and make my plate drop after I ate what I wanted. That way, Mama wouldn't get mad that I didn't eat it. It only worked some of the time. Mama was hip to my tricks and would apply the ten-second rule—if you drop your food on the floor, you have ten seconds to pick it up and eat it before the germs had a chance to make it inedible.

After dinner, we would shower and relax until it was time for bed. Typically, we would all go to Mama's room and lay down on her bed until about nine p.m. After that, we would get on our knees and say our prayers. If Mama had other foster youth staying there, she would call them into her room, if they weren't already in there watching television, so we could all pray as a family. She only fostered boys, as she didn't believe in mixing girls in the same household as boys, unless they were related. Most of the time, Mama led prayer, or she would tell everyone to repeat after her, so we all could learn how. Some nights, she would ask if anyone would like to lead. Peanut didn't like to pray; my other foster brothers were too shy to pray, so, I would. She would help me if I got stuck. Before I started, I asked everyone if they needed me to pray on anything specific. No one ever answered, but Mama always told me to pray for everything and to ask God to reunite her foster kids with their families. As prayed, I wondered if my mother couldn't get my siblings and me back was because no one had prayed for it. I would think hard

and would cut the prayer short by saying one of the first prayers that I
learned growing up: The Lord's Prayer.

> Our Father, who art in heaven
> Hallowed be thy Name,
> Thy Kingdom come,
> Thy will be done,
> On earth as it is in heaven.
> Give us this day our daily
> Bread.
> And forgive us our trespasses,
> As we forgive those
> who trespass against us.
> And lead us not into
> Temptation,
> But deliver us from evil.
> For thine is the kingdom,
> And the power; and the glory,
> For ever and ever. Amen.
> Matthew 6:9-13

We always went to bed saying that we loved each other with a hug.
I would get a kiss on the forehead. Peanut didn't like kisses. Right after,
we went to our room that we now shared since she started keeping more
children and attempted to go to sleep. Because so many children needed
a temporary placement until they went back with their biological parents, Mama would do her best to get as many children as she could.
We had a red bunk bed: the top was a twin bed, and the bottom queen.
Peanut would always sleep at the top, and I would sleep at the bottom.
Mama wouldn't let me sleep at the top after I woke up and hit my head
on the ceiling one night. I thought for a moment that I was too tall,

but, really, the ceilings weren't very high. Also, the fan in the center of the ceiling made weird noises, which would sometimes frighten me in the middle of the night. Peanut loved sleeping with the fan on, so some nights, I'd ask him to sleep with me.

In bed at night, Peanut and I would talk about our day, what we hoped for tomorrow; but we were never too sure if what we hoped for was going to happen. We would talk until we both fell asleep. It was comforting to know that someone who was related to me was staying with me. I've heard stories of how siblings get separated into different foster homes after being taken away from their parents. I understand the importance of ensuring that a child has a place to call "home," but I now know from experience that if there are other siblings involved, it's always best for the placement staff to try their best to place siblings with each other.

Schooling the System

Mama woke us up two hours before we had to leave for school just to make sure we got ready and made it to the bus stop on time. Peanut and I would have felt much better had she made us breakfast, but we knew she didn't have much time. She needed to get her rest, and she would always remind us that we should be thankful we received free breakfast and lunch at school—a program for students who lived in low-income homes. We chose our outfits for the entire week on Sunday nights, though Mama could change them if she thought what we'd set out was inappropriate for the weather or school.

The daily routine at school was always the same in that grade: Once mid-day came around, there was nap time, then story time, then snack time. Sometimes we'd get doughnuts from Krispy Kreme or have homemade treats, especially on Fridays. Parents often brought popcorn, candy, and Fruit Roll-ups for the entire class. I was always first in line to ensure I got one of each item. I also made sure to put my sleeping mat by the snack table for reassurance. I thought the parents with great jobs brought in the best treats for the class, like pizza, fruit bowls, individually bottled drinks, and assorted candy. Of course, those children would brag about how good their parents were and how they had many more snacks at home. I always thought they were only bragging just to get more friends, but it didn't steer me any different. I would still eat the snacks whether they were brought by my friends' parents or not.

Mama never signed to bring anything in for my classmates. She refused to take time off to bring in snacks, and she didn't want to waste her gas. At times, I was disappointed in her, because I wanted to prove to my friends that my family had just as much money as their family. Though the parents who did come more than likely purchased snacks out of the kindness of their hearts, I felt it must have meant that they had a lot of money. How else would they be able to afford such luxuries—the money for the snacks, the time off to bring them? I knew Mama couldn't afford to do that, so I didn't even bother to ask.

After snack time, we'd go to recess. Our teacher would allow us to go outside based on what color we were on. Green, for example, was for "excellent," a color I rarely received, so there was no need for me to ever rush out to the playground. I would sit and make noise until time went by. Finally, being one of the last ones called, I would run outside, racing toward the swing set with my friends who'd waited for me to be released. We didn't know how to swing by ourselves, so we took turns pushing each other.

After recess, we'd line up to prepare for dismissal. Our backpacks would already be outside by the main entrance of the school, so we wouldn't have to go back inside to get them. I would throw a fit, because our backpacks were lined up on the ground; I never liked to see my stuff on the ground, because Mama never liked for her purse to be on the ground, an old Southern superstition about being broke that had rubbed off on me too.

Peanut and I waited for the van that would transport us to after-school care to pick us up. It was like a funeral procession: long lines with buses identifiable from one another only by their numbers, kids hurrying onto them. Our van always came late. It was as if they forgot about their own youth. When they'd finally pick us up, we'd always hear the same excuse: "Sorry, lil' children. I got stuck by the train again, but I got some juice boxes and chips for each of you."

We would say, "Okay," and devour the snacks.

From that point forward, I realized that all an adult needed was snacks to keep a kid quiet.

At Golden Book after-school program, we had several different things we could do, from listening to someone read to us, to sleeping, to playing outside, to playing with arts and crafts, or helping to decorate the different rooms inside the building. I always chose to play outside, although I really wouldn't play. Instead, I would sit at the top of the big yellow slide for hours by myself waiting for Mama to pull up, so she could carry us home. While waiting, I'd watch two or three birds in the air fighting over food or two squirrels chasing each other up and down the oak tree. It reminded me of Peanut and me, how we would chase each other in the house or outside when we took each other's toys.

I always knew when Mama was coming to pick Peanut and me up. I would first hear the screeching of her van brakes. Then, I'd see the van approaching as she was turning into the daycare parking lot. I was always excited when she arrived, I'd run like a shooting bullet down the slide, through the red mulch, and over the wooden logs that the staff put there so we wouldn't jump and possibly hurt ourselves. I still jumped as I ran toward the van despite their reinforcements. They couldn't put me in time out anymore that day; my mama was there to get me.

By the time I got in the building from the back door, Mama would be coming up the stairs, so I'd go to the entrance door and be right there smiling and jumping. She'd open the door to give me hugs and kisses, and she'd ask about Peanut. I would say he was still playing outside and that he wanted to stay, never actually telling her that I'd never told him it was time to leave. When the staff members went to get him, he'd stomp his way inside, throwing a fit, but no one minded that. His clothes would be dirty and wet, despite knowing Mama would question his cleanliness. Mama didn't care about material things. She just didn't like using her washing machine and dryer all the time. If she did, the electric and water bill would go up. She tried to train us to not mess up our clothes, so we could re-use them later without having to wash them several times. Or she'd tell us the importance of keeping our clothes clean, because we never knew where we would go with her when we jumped in the van. All we were told to do was to "ride" and to not let anyone else know where we were going. She knew if we told others, they'd ask to come along, and she got tired of being everyone's taxi driver.

Through elementary school, I often found myself on either yellow or red status in class due to my behavior. I wasn't the best student, but I always tried to do my best. If I wasn't in time out, I would be getting a phone call home in the teacher's office. No one knew why I acted the way that I did. Sometimes I would throw crayons across the classroom, mess up someone else's work, or even play with the light switch, turning the lights on and off. I didn't even know what my problem was—at least, then I didn't. As time went on, it came to me: I wanted attention from everyone—I thought that getting my peers' attention through my careless actions would make me feel like I was important and that my presence was needed. During those days, I wasn't receiving the attention from Fannie, my biological mother, as I should have, so I thought I could get it from others.

As a troubled student in elementary school, I always looked for something to get caught up in. Then the phone calls home would follow. I had a burden on my heart, but I didn't know what it was for or about. As soon as I'd start to find my way onto the right track, I'd find myself back in emotional darkness. There was no light shining my way. I was internally disturbed and hurt.

During those days, it seemed as if everything was happening so fast, from my removal from my biological parents, to being adopted, to be a student in elementary school. Everyone expected me to go with the flow. I didn't agree to everything occurring around me. I felt uneducated since I didn't know what was going on; and I felt like an alien, because everywhere I went, I didn't know any faces or voices besides Peanut's. It was as if everyone that I met after the removal had an agenda for me. I didn't feel important, especially when I was identified by only a number when I first got in the foster care system; a number that didn't define who I really was; a number that was made so I could move forward in a process that I didn't ask to be in, like any other foster youth.

Everyone started seeing me as a defensive child. I wasn't purposely being rude or defensive; all I wanted was answers. I wanted to see my biological family more—my real mother, my real father, my real brothers and sisters. No one was going to stop me or get in the way of me seeing them, I thought, until I came to the realization that the consequences of my biological mother's actions and careless decisions prevented me from seeing her. She was often locked up because of her careless decisions or in a rehabilitation center. We would have to wait another eighteen months before we could begin visitation with her, because she was locked up in the county jail or in the state prison for poor decisions that she would soon regret while calling Peanut and I from the jail phone.

My father was never mentioned, because no one knew anything about him; it was as if he didn't exist. I didn't know his name or what he looked like. All I knew was that I had a father who may or may not claim me as his. I still wanted to meet him and for him to be the father figure in my life. Had he done that; I would have felt like he loved me. My brothers and sisters had relocated with another foster family who eventually adopted them or were out on their own because they were already eighteen years old, considered adults by law.

The only biological family members I knew were my grandma, who had a mind of her own, and my auntie, who was married. My grandma used to be an alcoholic during her young-adult years, so she knew what my mother was going through. Mama made the time to drop us off to visit with her as much as she could. My auntie had taken in my oldest brother until he was able to get going on his own. Peanut and I would visit her home periodically.

At school, teachers would always ask me, "What last name do you want me to call you? I see you have three last names." Before the adoption was finalized, my name was Jacari Edward Williams. Afterwards, it was changed to Jacari Etienne Williams-Harris. I didn't learn this until I was much older—and many of my personal documents reflect both names, though I am only one person. I felt embarrassed, because students would look at me and laugh or question why I had such a long name, as if I'd asked for it. I was the unforgettable student. Every student, faculty member, and teacher knew I wasn't like everyone else based on my name. Was I ashamed? Yes! But I wouldn't show it. I acted like everything was fine. Sometimes, I would make up a lie and tell them that my mother and father couldn't decide what my last name should be, so they added both to make it fair, though that wasn't the right answer. It was none of their business.

I'd go home and question Mama, "Why do Peanut and I have two middle names?"

Each time, she'd answer the same way that she'd named me all those names or that the court wouldn't let her change the names. But I just knew there was more to it. Whatever the real reasoning behind it, I was confused, and so were my teachers and anyone else who came across my name and files. I wanted to be like the other kids with one last name.

Third through fifth grade were the most memorable, joyous, and exciting years of my early school days. I was exposed to a lot, learning and experiencing new things. One of my most memorable times was during caterpillar season. All the teachers throughout the school had a cage for caterpillars so could experiment. First, we would learn the process of the butterfly life cycle.

It wasn't a fast process. The transformation of a caterpillar to an adult butterfly took time, gentle care, and patience, like my foster mama's methods. Seeing the process of a caterpillar transform to a butterfly may seem cliché, but there was a bigger story behind it: my story.

Now that I look back, there are many lessons a person can learn and apply to their own life from this natural metamorphosis. Sometimes, "breaking down" must occur for a restructuring to begin. A caterpillar must break down certain parts of themselves in order to take on another form. As I compare that to my life and the transition that occurred early on, I realize that I wouldn't be who I am today had I not been in the foster care system and adopted. The transition allowed me to experience a meaningful life with my new family. The second lesson that I learned was that everything we're taking in will be fuel and nourishment for our new form. As caterpillars eat, it provides nourishment that is stored and will be used later (as an adult). I had to start trusting the process and the experiences that I went through so that I wouldn't make the same mistakes as my biological mother and father.

Entering middle school, I didn't attend the local school or the middle school that Peanut, my cousin Nancy, and many of my friends went to. The transit system for schools had changed, which caused a reduction of pick-ups and drop-offs in my area. Yet another system interrupted my life and switched things, so I'd have to adapt to something new.

Mama heard about a new charter school that would open before the academic year, so she thought it best for me to go there instead. During that time, she had a foster child named Carl, and she informed him too about the charter school She wanted him to attend there as well. I really wanted to be with my brother, cousins, and elementary-school friends, since they were all going to the same middle school, but the school wouldn't approve my enrollment due to the new school zone map that was released. Mama then enrolled Carl and me in the charter school, believing that we would be able to build better characters for ourselves there as well as get a quality education. Mama wanted Peanut to attend as well, but she also didn't want him to transfer schools and disrupt his education journey.

As I look back over that school year, I realize now the absolute worst educational decisions were made for me. For one, we had to be in uniform every day. Our pants had to be ironed with a crease, our collars wrinkle free, shirts tucked into our navy, black, or khakis slacks. I hated the yellow polo. It was dull with the school's logo embroidered on it. I wouldn't eat sometimes during my lunch period, because I was clumsy and didn't want to spill food on my clothes. If I did, Mama would rant about eating properly and taking care of my stuff, because every time she washed the school uniform, it would shrink, and the color would fade—which was against the dress-code policy. At the beginning of the year, she purchased two polos, two pairs of black or navy-blue shoes, and the pants we needed for school, all of which were very expensive, for Carl and me both. I told Mama I didn't like looking like everyone else, because they weren't like me. They hadn't been through the things I had gone through and still was going through.

After a few weeks in the school, I finally got the answer to the question that I'd asked my teacher every morning when she started class: "Why do we have to wear uniforms?" I thought she was going to be a smart aleck and educate me on the history of uniforms and why some schools implemented a uniform policy. Then, I thought she was going to use some big words that I wouldn't even be able to pronounce. But, instead, she gave a short, detailed and meaningful response.

"Jacari, we wear uniforms so we can look unified, and because we know that some parents can't afford to purchase school clothes and shoes for their children. So, with a uniform policy in place, we can mitigate possible bullying from students who are accustomed to wearing the same clothes repeatedly."

I felt bad for asking the question after she answered it, because many of the students started to look around the room to see if they could identify which students couldn't afford clothing, not to degrade them, but to offer some of their clothes.

The next week, we started an anonymous clothing drive for our peers who were in need. All in all, I was happy that after asking the question and starting the clothing drive we were able to position our minds to be more giving and understanding—that we must be more caring to those around us. Although this was one of my favorite moments at school, that didn't change my behavior or opinion about anything else.

I made many friends but that didn't stop me from getting into trouble. At this point, I loved testing my teachers by coming to class late and mocking them as they lectured. I was the class clown and wanted everything to go my way. I had only two teachers, which was weird based on what I heard growing up about middle school. As the other middle schoolers around town had a minimum of six teachers per academic year, one for each of their courses. Since the charter school was new with a small starting class, everything was downsized. I knew I wouldn't get the middle school experience I always overheard Peanut talking about with his friends.

Eventually, I started doing my own thing. If I didn't like the lesson that was being taught, I would color or write in my journal. The teachers were trying so hard to keep me engaged, but eventually I'd end up in the principal's office. Unlike other kids, I liked going to the principal's office. The principal couldn't handle me. She thought I was a stubborn smart aleck. I had something to say about everything. If she asked me what was going on in my mind, I would tell her, "The same thing that is going on in yours."

What boiled me the most was when she would say, "Young man, your mother and I will talk about your behavior." It upset me, because she thought she knew my family, but anyone could lie on a piece of paper. She had no idea what can of worms she had opened. She tried to counsel me and talk through situations. Ultimately, she wanted to understand why I acted out so much. She thought she knew me so well until I went off on her. By the conclusion of my time in her office, I was either on in-school suspension or suspended from going to school altogether. That didn't stop me, though. I would laugh at the poor lady and tell her that I wouldn't get in trouble with my mother, because I hadn't seen her in a while, though I knew that Mama was going to whoop me to sleep.

On the way to school, while riding the school bus; we would go through different neighborhoods to pick up students. My favorite neighborhood was in the same community that the school was at. This neighborhood is the one that ultimately got me interested in housing and development as I got older. The houses weren't average in look or style. I didn't see any mobile homes or patches in the dark green grass. I couldn't afford them, and I didn't believe that I *would* ever afford them. Yet I would often ask Mama about them because she wanted a real house. We had high hopes that we would be blessed with a similar house one day. Some Saturday mornings, Mama take us to the homes in the school's neighborhood to participate in open houses. Entering the entrance of the new built homes, all our mouths would drop in admiration. We'd walk in every room, touch every wall and begin decreeing and declaring that God would give us a better home.

One day, a national television show on ABC Network, Extreme Makeover Home Edition, came to town. For years, Mama, Peanut, and watched this TV show on Sunday evenings after we ate a big dinner. This show's overall purpose was to help families in need, whether it was for more space in a house, to build accessible areas for handicapped people, or to build a new house altogether. The TV host, Ty Pennington, would first give background history on the family. Some of their descriptions reminded me of my own family.

The day I found out the show was coming to Tallahassee, I prayed that they would come to my house. We had applied on their website. I took pictures of all the work that needed to be done around the house. It had gotten so bad that the roof was starting to cave in when it rained. We'd place a bucket on the floor under the leak, so no one would slip or fall. Once the bucket got full, Peanut and I would take turns dumping out the water.

No one knew which family would be chosen, but we counted the days until their arrival. I would set my alarm clock before the sun rose and walk back and forth to the living room window, peeping out to see if any trucks were coming.

On the fifth morning, Mama and I found out that the TV show had selected a home less than a mile away from us. Although we weren't the family chosen, it was good that one of the kids from my school's family was. The show featured the story of the Kadzis family– George, Barbara, their biological son and six special-needs adopted children. The feature was great publicity for the charter school, which had recently opened, and for the act of adopting vulnerable youth.

Each day afterwards, I would watch the local news to find out what was happening with the house. We could see semi-trucks lined up on the side of the road, ready to enter the neighborhood to drop off supplies for the construction. The night before the new house was revealed to the family, I asked Mama if we could go to the revealing. She told me "no," and when I asked why, she told me that she couldn't miss a day of work.

I didn't let that stop me, though. I was determined to see it.

That evening, we sat at the dinner table eating my favorite Hamburger Helper meal that Mama had cooked: beef stroganoff, sweet green peas, and a slice of white bread. I was eating quickly, trying to think of how I could get to the location of the new house. I knew I couldn't say anything to Peanut, because he would tell. I had to make it seem like I was going to school. After dinner, I went down the hall to take a shower. Mama came and knocked on the door, yelling for me to, "Get out!"- I knew I was going to get in trouble.

"You are wasting all of the hot water, and now Peanut and I have to wait until the water gets back hot!" she yelled at me.

It'd totally slipped my mind how long I was in the shower, because I was daydreaming about how much I would enjoy the festivities. I hurriedly turned off the water and went to my room to plan more. A few minutes later, I was told to turn off my light and go to sleep. I did as I was told, but I couldn't sleep. I started thinking of all the possible ways I would be punished once I got caught, because I knew getting caught was inevitable.

The next morning, I woke up extra early, so I could prepare everything that I needed for the day. Mama had a breathing machine that she used every night, so I knew she wouldn't hear me walking through the kitchen packing snacks for my day. Though the bus came at six-thirty, I decided to turn off the alarm clock Mama used, which was set for five-thirty. I hoped she would oversleep. Fifteen minutes after six, I ran to her room, shouting, "It's past our wake-up time!" She jumped up and turned off her breathing machine and told me to wake up Peanut and get dressed for school. We heard her questioning herself why she didn't hear the alarm sound.

I hoped Mama would cancel taking us to school since she knew we would be late, but no! She called her sister, our neighbor, to take us to the late bus. After arriving at the bus stop, I told the her she could leave and drop Peanut off because school started a little earlier than mine. That way, she wouldn't see me not get on the bus. She asked many questions, as any concerned mother would, and I answered them wisely. When she finally left, I ran to the store to get Gatorades, because I knew I would need to be hydrated throughout the day. While checking out with the cashier, I saw the school bus passing by. A part of me felt terrible, but I was more excited than anything.

Then I became very nervous, because I knew I was in a lot of trouble. I kind of wanted to call my Mama and tell her what I'd done. But then I wanted to keep going, because I'd never been on TV before—it made me feel better about my decision.

On my way to the house reveal, I weaved through the woods, so I wouldn't be seen. Cars were lined up for miles in all directions. I overheard bystanders say they'd camped out on the outskirts of the grounds of the house, so they would be able to get a good view. When I was told that I could enter the neighborhood, there were thousands of people crowded in front of the house, waiting for the family to arrive. It was a beautiful day, as the sun beamed down on our foreheads. There was loud music, food vendors, and games on every corner. The Extreme Makeover street team was interviewing people, asking them to volunteer to put décor and plants in the house.

I started getting nervous and began patting my pockets, thinking that my phone was vibrating. Sometimes, I would glance at it to make sure I didn't receive any missed calls or texts. I was thirteen at the time and had a Virgin Mobile phone that I'd purchased by saving up my allowance for over a year. When we started receiving an allowance, we got twenty-five dollars a month. Some months Mama wouldn't be able to give out allowances because she had extra children in her care. Still, I saved about a hundred and seventy-five dollars and I got the best phone I could afford. Though it didn't have many features, I was happy to just have a phone.

As hours went by on the day of the reveal of the home, I started receiving phone calls back to back, from numbers I didn't recognize. I ignored them, praying that family or friends weren't in the area, because if they were, I would be in more trouble.

Finally, the time came! The family arrived in a fine black stretch limousine. The show producers and media representatives were set in place to capture the special moment that we'd all been waiting for. When the family got out of the car, we started chanting, "Move that bus! Move that bus!" A few seconds later, we heard the bus positioned in front of the home to keep it hidden start, then it moved down the street. Behind it stood a beautiful two-story home that had been built in seven days. The atmosphere around the house and family was breathtaking—it was almost like magic.

When I turned around, I immediately saw faculty and staff members from my charter school. I was startled. I knew the outcome would be bad. Yet, I was able to witness a historical moment for a family that truly deserved this new home; this became especially clear when because George Kadiz died about forty-eight hours after his family moved in.

Walking in the other direction, I maneuvered my way through the crowd. As soon as I thought I'd gotten away from staff from my school, an altercation broke out between two men. *Darn it,* I thought to myself. There was no way for me to get away now. All eyes started to turn toward me, and I moved to avoid being seen by anyone I knew. Onlookers hissed and yelled, because I was pushing through the crowd aggressively. The ABC film team came back to film the crowd after they all agreed to be on television, so they soon left me alone to start cheering for the Kadiz family.

At the exit gate, a white Ford Crown Victoria trimmed in gold sat parked. I thought something was strange, because there were no other cars parked there, and there was a "NO Parking" sign right by it. The rear door was open, but no one was in the back seat. I continued to head towards the exit gate, anyway, just trying to make it away from there. As soon as I walked by the car, I heard a very loud voice saying; "Get in the car! Get in the car right now and put on your seat belt!"

From the sound of the voice, I wanted to die and come back to life. I knew it was my school's principal. I followed her demands precisely, knowing that I couldn't run far without her catching me. As I got in the car, my hands and feet started to go numb. I didn't know what to say, and I couldn't even position my lips to utter a word, because I knew I was in hot water. Mama would be contacted. I was going to get my butt tore up that night. Being that I was adopted, in Mama's eyes, she could discipline me however she wanted as my legal guardian. In comparison, if s a foster youth was in trouble in our home, she would ground him or call his case worker. Mama wouldn't dare whoop a foster youth in her care unless they had been with her for years—which rarely happened. She knew the consequences if she were reported to a case manager.

The drive back to the school was worse than a road trip across the U.S. She took the longest route possible, so she could stop by McDonald's and drop off mail at the post office. The wait at McDonald's was unbearable. Between the long drive-thru line, the broken ice cream machine, her having to use the bathroom after getting a smoothie in lieu of the ice cream she wanted, I was getting impatient. Her car was cold from the air conditioner on maximum cold. Before leaving the parking lot, she left me in the car as she went inside to use the bathroom. I could have left the car and ran home as she entered the restaurant, but I didn't want to get in any more trouble. When she came back into the car, she popped in a CD and started playing country music. I laughed and started playing gospel music that was on my phone. I didn't have earphones, because I didn't have enough allowance to purchase them, and Mama got tired of replacing them for me every time I lost them. Eventually, she demanded that I turn off my phone and give it to her, because she viewed me listening to music as disrespectful while she had her music on.

When we finally got to school, the school safety officer—the principal's son—escorted me to the main office. I couldn't take him seriously, because he looked as if he'd jump if I said, "Boo!" I overheard the staff complaining and questioning how I ended up at the house makeover. I wanted to give them a piece of my mind, because they'd been there as well. However, I just sat in the corner laughing because they couldn't figure out how I got there. They asked me, of course, but I wouldn't tell them. I had already done what I wanted to; now I had to face the consequences of my actions.

Since I wouldn't comply and answer their questions, I was escorted to the principal's office so Mama could come to pick me up. Fifteen minutes past four, I heard Mama coming up the stairs, telling everyone that she was going to make an example out of me. I started smirking, because during those times, I thought I was bold knowing well and well that behind closed doors she was going to whoop me.

She cut her eyes at me and began apologizing to the staff as if she owed them an apology. She didn't even like them, but as the old folks would say, "Don't ever let the right hand know what the left hand is doing." My mama was doing just that. After signing the release forms, she pinched me on my arm and told me to go downstairs and wait by the car. The look on my face showed her how I was really feeling; she knew that I didn't like to be pinched. After we both got in the car, we rode home in silence. All the windows were up, the AC was off, and the radio was muted. I heard nothing but the engine going.

Once we got home, she told me to go to my room, close the door, and to not come out until I was told. I did just that and didn't hear anything else about the situation. I figured she couldn't place the blame on me since our neighbor hadn't made sure I made it on the bus.

HEALED WOUNDS

Over one summer, Mama enrolled me into a camp that ultimately changed my course of life. We didn't know what the future would hold; the only thing Mama knew was that she was signing me up so that I'd have enrichment activities throughout the week instead staying home doing nothing. Two to three times a week the camp would go on a field trip, either to a museum, skating rink, fun station, or a theme park. On Fridays we would always go skating along with other similar summer camps. It was a great time to meet new people, have fun, and compete in race skating with other people we'd never met.

One Friday, I competed in a race grouped by age, the ten, eleven, and twelve-year-old race, as I had just turned twelve. It would be my last time skating for years.

As they called my group to move to the starting line, boys who weren't a part of the camp ran to the front of the line. Immediately, I knew they would be a challenge, being so rough before the competition had even started. After the referees made the last call for anyone who wanted to participate, they went over the rules and regulations. I was in the middle of everyone, nervous because I was the only Black boy competing in the race. I could tell that everyone had already counted me out by how they were shoving and laughing, but I was determined to win.

The group of boys weren't paying attention to the referees; they were horse playing and debating on who would win between their group.

The countdown began. As soon as we heard the whistle, everyone started racing to get to the front. I was going as fast as I could but was distracted by all the noise from the crowd cheering. Before I could go around the first corner, one of the dudes who was being rough tried to cut me off and tripped me. That was it.

I didn't want to open my eyes, and I couldn't move. All I could do was lie on the hard marble floor and cry. I had fallen flat on my face, body aching with pain; I didn't know what to do but cry for Mama.

The camp director came rushing over and asked all the students to give me some breathing room. I couldn't hear much. It seemed as if my hearing was going in and out; I was in so much pain. The staff tried to get me up, but my body had shut down. They tried to turn me over on my back, but that only caused me to start screaming and crying more. They realized that my leg was swelling as the seconds went by. I overheard a staff member stating that they were going to get a wheelchair to help me up. But they didn't know how to pick me up without hurting me, so they called the paramedics. Minutes later, the paramedics arrived and transported me to the nearest hospital. As soon as we got there, I heard Mama in the background asking the doctor if I was alright. All they said was that it would take some time for me to heal.

I was rushed to the X-ray room to see if I needed surgery. When we got to the room, they asked me to move slowly out of the bed they'd wheeled me in on to check my entire leg and see how badly it was swollen. But that wasn't happening. I could barely walk. Mama was right by my side encouraging me, telling me that I needed to trust the doctor's process. I wanted to, but it hurt too much.

Hours later, I was rolled out of the hospital in a wheelchair. I had a femur shaft fracture. A blue cast covered my right leg, from my foot to my femur bone. I didn't think I would be able to live another day.

I was still angry. I couldn't believe someone had tripped me just to try to win a stupid competition. It reminded me of the pain I'd felt when the separation happened—my biological mother making mistakes, but I was the one who had to suffer. I am the one who had to go through a system that identified me by a number. I started taking pain medicine to reduce the pain in my legs, just as I was given toys and candy to do away with the tears that came during the separation.

I remembered the Pastor saying, "But those who hope in the Lord will renew their strength. They will soar on wings like eagles; they will run and not grow weary, they will walk and not faint," coming from Isaiah 40:31. I went home and studied the scripture, trying to apply it to my life, but it was hard. The incident had taken a toll on me. I even began calling out to my Heavenly Father, seeking answers, questioning him, wondering why I had to deal with the sharp pains that ran through my upper right leg from time to time. I begged him to equip me with strength. Sometimes I wondered if he was even listening to me. It seemed as if I didn't get any response to any of the questions, I'd asked him. I felt handicapped. I couldn't take a shower alone, couldn't cook my own food. If I stood up for too long, I would end up being carried to the bed, weeping. I felt the pain all over, but it was only in my upper leg. I was enrolled in the summer camp at my school, but I had to sit out and watch Mama's money be thrown down the drain. Mama ultimately decided I wouldn't go back to summer camp just to sit out.

The more I thought of that field trip—a trip I'd almost got banned from attending due to my attitude—the more I became angered. I couldn't understand why I was the one going through this abnormal pain. I wasn't messing with anyone to deserve being hurt. I was just hanging out with my summer camp friends who knew that I was one of the best skaters in the summer camp. But that day, I learned that you can be great one day, and another day someone could take your spot.

I had weekly scheduled appointments with my doctor and physical therapist for the first three weeks after getting my cast to learn to walk with my cast and crutches. The therapist worked me until I was worn out. I'd tell Mama I wouldn't go, but I still went.

The therapist was short, long-haired, pretty, and young, but her demands for me to move and walk across the room in a timely fashion made her seem ugly to me. I kept asking questions like, "Have you ever broken a bone? Have you ever had a cast?" She would laugh each time and never answer my questions, though I was serious in asking them.

Before I got hurt, I did most of the housework, but now the tables had turned. I was able to relax and watch my brothers cook and clean daily. In my eyes, it was revenge. I could finally get a break from chores, but I couldn't do anything else.

After a few weeks, I was tired of being dependent, tired of waiting for people to do things for me when they felt like it, so I started doing things for myself. If I wasn't cooking my own food, I was washing clothes or trying to clean the house. Each morning, I got up, cooked breakfast, browsed the internet or went outside and enjoyed nature until Mama got home. She was usually upset with me. I was supposed to be on bed rest with my leg propped up on pillows, but I was doing everything else but that.

I can still hear Mama saying, "Boy, if you don't sit down somewhere, your leg will never get better." I laughed whenever she said that. That is, until one night I was washing clothes, when I reached up for detergent, jerked back too fast, and suddenly couldn't move an inch. It felt just like the day I was on the floor at the skating rink. I began to cry and call for help. Mama, the therapist, Peanut and Aymin came to see what the issue was. I didn't know what to say. I could only lay my head on the washer. I didn't want to move; it felt almost as if my leg would fall off if I did.

My cast wasn't supporting me; it was getting too loose. I knew it was time for a new one. I thought I could wait another week to go to the follow-up appointment. Mama went to get my crutches, but she couldn't find them. I told them to call the paramedics, but Mama didn't see the point when I was the one who'd disobeyed the doctor's orders. She was right; I could blame only myself. I got more upset because I hadn't listened to Mama when she told me that I needed to relax. I started asking for forgiveness because I didn't know what else to do. The therapist thought that giving me pain medication would help. She was right.

The next morning, I was driven to the doctor, so I could get another cast. The doctor said I'd been moving too fast and re-hurt myself. I had about eight weeks left to wear it, so I was told that I really needed to follow directions, or I would need surgery. I knew I had to change my ways, because I didn't want to go through with that.

At times I would go in the stores with Mama and drive the handicap carts. I was so excited, because I'd always wanted to drive one, and I finally had the opportunity. I would drive around the entire store until it was time to go. As the weeks went on, I could walk more and do things for myself. By week eight, I went back to the doctor's office, and he took the cast off. I could have taken the cast home with me as a souvenir, but it smelled like sour sweat. Plus, I didn't want to be reminded of what I had just gone through.

After having my cast off for a while, I began to think of all the people who had similar pain. It may not have been from a broken bone, but from someone or something else in life. Whatever it may have been, I was a testimony that God could heal me to be even better than the condition I was in before the accident. All I needed was a little faith and patience.

SUMMER AT AUNT CHERRYE'S

The summer of 2009, I stayed with one of Mama's sisters, because she needed help around the house. Mama guaranteed she would take good care of me. She lived in St. Petersburg, Florida, about four hours away from our home. I loved cleaning, so I knew I would fit in. Also, the idea of staying in another city was great, but what I didn't do was inquire with other family members about how it would be to stay with this specific aunt. I was twelve years old, and I didn't think it could be that bad.

The day before I left, I overheard Mama on the phone saying that she hoped I would come back disciplined. I couldn't understand how she thought that someone who I'd never stayed with before could discipline me in a few short months, but, nevertheless, I went on.

Mama didn't like driving long distances, so she got her niece to drop me off on her way to Tampa. As soon as we made it to St. Petersburg, we stopped by McDonald's to get me something to eat. I remember her niece saying, "I'm getting you this because I know you will not eat out with Aunt Cherrye, because she doesn't drive." My mouth dropped open in disappointment because Mama hadn't told me this part.

The thought that I would have to stay inside made me nervous. I began to have second thoughts about staying with her, because I knew I would get bored quickly. I was too afraid to ask to stay with the niece until she went back to Tallahassee, so I sat in silence as we made our way to my auntie's house. When we arrived, my aunt was leaning on her van, waiting for me in the early afternoon in her pink nightgown, slippers, and hair-bonnet. Her garage was open and a complete mess. All I could see was furniture, boxes, and grey bins filled with clothes, shoes, and household items. I was concerned for her well-being. She was too old to have as much stuff as she did and not be organized. A true hoarder. I already knew the garage would be a project that I would be working on while staying with her.

By the look on her face, I could tell she was happy to see me, or glad that she wouldn't be staying by herself. When Mama's niece left, my aunt walked me to the room I'd be staying in. It was the room that her adopted son had stayed in before he was removed to a behavioral center due to a disability. I had heard all about him and how he was spoiled, which was no issue; but when she started to write down rules for me as it pertained to his belongings, I became bothered. I couldn't use the house computer to search the web, because it was his computer. The Wii couldn't be touched, and if I changed the station on his radio, she would have a fit. Before I could even ask why I couldn't use his belongings, especially being that he hadn't been there in a while, she already had her lips fixed with the answer.

"No, because if you break it, you don't have the money to replace it, so leave it alone." She made me feel as if I was clumsy or didn't know how to use the devices. I was most irritated about not being able to use the computer to surf the web. I didn't see the issue with wanting to learn more and understand why things are the way they are. I knew I could learn a lot from reading; when I looked at her bookshelf, the only genre of books she had was about love and marriage. I didn't care for that at my age. Instead, she bought me a one-thousand-piece puzzle of New York City—she believed it would keep me busy and thinking.

When it came to watching TV, I could only watch what she wanted in her living room. She didn't believe in having multiple TVs in the house. So, on the days I got tired of lying in bed, I'd sit on the living room floor with my back against the couch and watch whatever she was watching. She knew every news channel that her cable provider had. When one news channel went to commercial, she'd change the channel to another news show. Anytime there was breaking news, she'd turn the volume up as if she expected to hear something different. Then, she'd go to the front room and peep through the curtains to see if she saw anything. I never knew what she was looking for, but I would laugh every time.

In fact, I laughed at almost everything she did. It aggravated the hell out of her. She couldn't understand why I laughed so much. In all honesty, I don't even know why I was laughing. It bothered her so much that she would just go to her room and shut her door. Before doing that, she'd yell at me, "Lil' boy, let me tell you something. I'm not your mama, and I'll send you back on the Greyhound if you keep on keepin' on." I'd stare at her and burst out in tears, laughing. She thought my feelings would be hurt had she sent me back home.

One thing she was good at was cooking. Mama told her that I'd recently gone vegetarian after completing a project for my health and wellness class that required me to learn how meat was processed. When my auntie told me to make a list of all the foods that I liked to eat, I expected her to inform her daughter, who picked up groceries, to get everything that was on the list. Most of the items I listed were junk food, which she didn't believe in getting. The woman cooked three meals a day, unless we had leftovers. She didn't believe in throwing away food.

One time—when she was cooking dinner—she decided to add pieces of meat in the pot with the vegetables she was going to serve for dinner. When fixing my plate, she tried to sneak and scoop the meat out, but I already knew that trick because Mama tried it when serving dinner, and I wasn't having it. I knew the meat flavor was cooked in with the vegetables, so I wasn't going to eat it. When she gave me the plate, I asked if the vegetables were cooked separately from the meat, and she tried to convince me that they were. I already knew the truth, I just wanted to know if she would be honest with me. I waited until she was done eating before I threw the vegetables away. I went to bed only having eaten white rice and a biscuit. I couldn't understand why she thought it was okay to let me go to bed without eating enough to carry me over throughout the night, but she wasn't putting up with my dietary needs.

Before she went to bed, she cleaned the kitchen; she didn't believe in going to bed with a dirty kitchen. For some reason, she decided to look through the trash. Then, all I heard was yelling and the trash can being bang around. I couldn't interpret exactly what she was saying—or I just didn't care. What I could understand when she yelled that I was no longer allowed to take out the trash. It didn't bother me. Instead, it gave me a reason to purposely make trash, since I couldn't do anything else. She walked closer to the room I was in, calling me "ungrateful" and a "spoiled brat," because I didn't eat certain foods.

About a month into my stay, she got tired of me wasting food, so she stopped cooking for me altogether. I had to make my own food. While making it, she stood over me watching my every move, criticizing the way that I cooked. I would smirk and say slick remarks, so she would know that I didn't care. That didn't stop her, though. She continued complaining and trying to tell me what to do and how to do it. When she decided to cook for me again, it was because she got tired of me overusing her gas; she made rice and sweet peas. I knew she was up to something, because I didn't see the Uncle Ben's rice box. That was the only white rice I would eat, since that's the rice Mama would always cook back home. She, instead, cooked rice that came from a plastic bag—the same rice she told me she didn't like to eat. I don't know why she was making it harder for the both of us, but she persisted. There weren't any signs that she'd learned her lesson as it pertained to my vegetarian diet. I never knew if she just didn't think I should be allowed to pick and choose what I wanted to eat, since I wasn't an adult, or if she just wanted to be stubborn.

Another time, before it was time to eat dinner, she told me to go to the bathroom and wash my hands. When I returned to the kitchen after washing my hands, I saw a plate filled with slimy white rice, sweet peas and chicken wings. I thought it was her plate, but there were two plates on the table fixed the same way. My entire mood changed in a matter of seconds. I was not going to eat anything on that plate. I told her, "If you expect me to eat chicken, knowing that I'm a vegetarian, you're going to see what I'm about."

She looked at me and laughed, then said, "This is my house, my food, and my rules, so if you're staying here, you're going to eat what I cook, or you won't eat at all."

I was determined to show her that I wasn't the one to play with, especially when it came to me eating. I threw the entire plate in the trash, went to my room, and slammed the door. While I was laying down, I overheard her on the phone talking to Mama, telling her what I had done and how disrespectful of a child I was. My aunt then called me to get the phone to speak to my mama. On my way back to the kitchen, I shouted, "She can't make me eat chicken either, so calling her served no purpose." When I took the phone from her, she jumped at me and murmured a comment. I couldn't hear what she said, but I am sure it was nothing less than petty.

While on the phone, Mama told me to get my act together and eat what I could before my aunt stopped feeding me altogether. By that time, I was ready to go home. I wanted to go where I felt most happy, where I could be myself without anyone beating down my throat. I knew I couldn't take any more of my aunt's rules and excessive cleaning responsibilities. I couldn't even sleep in except on Saturdays. Early in the mornings, right when the sun started rising, she had me in her flower bed picking weeds, cutting limbs, raking, and putting the leaves in a black trash bag. I don't know if I should be thankful that she made me get up before it got too hot outside to finish the task at hand or thankful that she brought me bottled water every other hour when she came to check on me.

After cleaning the front yard, I would then go to the back porch and straighten it up. Sometimes, I didn't know where to start, because she had her son's items in bins. I didn't know what she wanted me to go through, so I took it upon myself to throw the items away I thought were outdated. She didn't know I was throwing things away until she asked me to get an item for her that I had put in the trash. I was too afraid to tell her that it was in the trash, so she went looking for it, then came back yelling when she realized it was no longer there. She then called her daughter and reported to her what I'd done. I just laughed it off, because I knew it would aggravate her. I figured that her daughter knew she was a hoarder as well, which is why she never mentioned anything to me when she came over.

The next day, my aunt told me that she no longer wanted me on her back porch. Instead, she had extra work for me to do in the front yard and in her backyard garden. The garden wasn't big enough to harvest enough food for one person. There were a few plants, and the soil wasn't healthy. I got the shovel and made the garden wider, so that I could plant the seeds I'd found in a bin on her porch. If I hadn't found them, she wouldn't have known they were there. After planting them, I went on to play on her son's wooden swing set. Most times, she didn't know I was on it, because I would play after we ate lunch. I knew she would take her noon-day nap. If she woke from her nap, she'd yell at me through her window to tell me to get off. Even though her son was heavier than me, she was convinced I would be the one to break the swing.

As time went on, my attitude got worse and her responses made it no better. I started doing things just because I felt like it. I got tired of lying in bed, cleaning, watching the news, and trying to put together a one-thousand-piece puzzle that didn't have all the pieces to it. At night, she'd go to bed right when the sun went down. I took that time to sneak on her computer to play Fun Brain, an educational website. For several nights, I was up to the wee hours of the morning playing the game. One night, my aunt woke up and caught me, and all hell broke loose.

It was around one a.m. when I heard her moving around in bed. I couldn't tell whether she was changing sleeping positions or getting up to go to the restroom adjoining her room; whatever she was doing, I didn't think to go to my room until the noise went away. Instead, I dimmed the lighting on the computer monitor so she wouldn't see that it was on, just in case she opened her room door to look around the house. After a few moments of silence, I went back to playing Fun Brain. Before I knew it, a flashlight was pointed in my direction. My aunt stood by her door beaming the flashlight on me. When I realized I was caught, I started to shake. I knew how she got when I touched things that didn't belong to me, especially the computer.

Before I knew it, she was walking toward me with a broom, yelling and demanding me to get up and go to bed. I was trying to save the game and log out before she came over, so I wouldn't get hit with the broom just in case she did swing it. As soon as the game was saved, she hit me with the broom handle. I grabbed it and tried to shove it away, but she started throwing anything in her reach at me, so I wouldn't come in her direction. I ran to my room and slammed the door. The next morning, I woke up to find the computer on the floor outside her bedroom door. She didn't have any breakfast cooked, and all she told me to do was start packing my stuff because I was going home. I wasn't mad. At that point, I thought it was best for me to go home, because had I not, destruction was sure to happen in the coming days.

About two days later, a family friend came to get me. I haven't been back to her house since. However, to this day, we are in contact. When I see her at family functions, she always brings up the time I stayed with her and tells me how much I've matured since then. Sometimes, she even has the audacity to ask if I would stay with her again.

I always respond with a fake smile and a kind, "No, thank you."

After staying with her, I realized that you can't just stay with anyone. No matter if they are friends or family—you must really know the person you are staying with, what they believe in, their personal views on living conditions, and things that trigger them. I don't agree with the way she acted; I was just a child, still learning who I really was. Contrary to my experience living with her, she has a wonderful soul and means good whenever you are on her good side. I love her lots, just wouldn't torture myself again by staying with her.

BRIDGING THE GAP

B y the time I was fifteen, Peanut was often in and out of the house due to his behavior. He stayed with our older adoptive brother, Aymin who had an apartment with his girlfriend. She thought that he'd do better if he had an older man around him—like a father figure, but that hypothesis failed. Peanut eventually dropped out of high school his junior year and started working at different fast-food restaurants. I wonder how much easier his life would have been had he finished high school. As his youngest brother, and us placed in the same foster home, I thought he would at least finish what he started, his education, high school, to encourage me to follow in his footsteps.

Though I was upset about his decision not to continue high school, I was grateful he was in my life. I've always thought that's the best thing our case worker could have done, keeping siblings together, no matter where we moved to. Though I had other siblings, and Peanut and I didn't see each other as much when he was in and out of the house, my life wouldn't have gone as well as it did in foster care without Peanut.

We looked totally different from each other. He was light skinned, and I was dark skinned. But it didn't matter what color we were, because color never existed in our eyes. What we knew was that we'd started the journey together and that we would get through any obstacle that came about. Some people couldn't believe that he was my brother since we didn't have physical traits in common. What we had was the same biological mother. His father was never around; Peanut never met him.

I never knew why I still hadn't heard from my biological father either. When I began to question his absence to both my biological and adoptive mothers, I could never seem to get a straight answer. My biological mother made excuses and said she hadn't heard from him in years. My adoptive mom told me she hadn't heard from him since I was a toddler. I had never seen a picture of him, nor did I even receive a phone call from him, so I assumed he had died. That was my best solution to fix the void within. I didn't feel bad about my assumption, because no one ever told me any different.

Sometimes I wonder how I would have turned out had my father taken us his children into his care custody. I'm sure he didn't regret his decision for not taking us in. He didn't care. He was doing his own thing, laying up with other women, getting them pregnant, leaving them, and working dead-end jobs. He never paid child support, and I am sure he never intended to do so, either.

I wonder what could have been going through his mind. He knew he had other children in the world in addition to the ones he was taking care of with his new girlfriend, yet he only showed up to two visitations to see my two sisters, older brother and me—his four children with my biological mother. By only appearing for two visitations, the court declared months later that my father was never active in my life and didn't have a close relationship with me or his other children.

The seasons gradually changed. The colorful bright orange and yellow leaves started to crinkle and wither, and the night air's cool breeze flowed more. My favorite holiday, Thanksgiving, was right around the corner, and my entire family was excited about the cruise to Cozumel, Mexico we were taking for my birthday. Some of us had never been on a cruise before, so we were both excited and afraid. Even though Peanut wasn't living with us, Mama wanted him to come with us to experience a new country. We spent countless hours researching the cruise ship, looking at all the things we could do. We watched people share their experience on YouTube. We also created a budget together. That way, we would have enough money for excursions and fancy dining. Of course, Mama would be the one doing all the spending, but we wanted to do a lot, so we had to ensure she could afford it.

Two days before our departure, I packed my clothes. Mama printed a checklist to ensure we had everything. Shortly after, my biological mother called and asked for Peanut and me to meet her and Pop, her husband, at our bus stop, so she could give me my birthday present. Her smile was much brighter. She had on a nice Michael Kors outfit, and she had gained a little weight. She also wanted to give Peanut some money to carry with him. She wasn't allowed to come to our house out of respect and for security reasons, so we always met her at the bus stop or gas station.

I opened my gifts: a watch, camera, thirty dollars, and some socks. I was grateful, believing she was still trying to do better to make up for those times when she couldn't do anything for us. Peanut got thirty dollars. Before saying our goodbyes, she repeatedly told us to be safe and to watch out for strangers. She then went on to tell us about how a recent cruise goer had gotten lost at sea, so she didn't think it was right for us to go. Our minds were already made. Nothing was going to stop us from going. Besides, we knew Mama wouldn't allow anyone to do anything to us. Peanut ended the conversation as he would always do when he got tired of talking, so we could return home. As soon as the car she was in drove off, we raced each other home to share with Mama what our biological mother had given.

After sharing with Mama, it was time for us to prepare for bed. We had to be up before sunrise to head to Orlando to meet other members of our family going on the cruise as well. After saying our prayers, we went to bed. No one slept, though. I heard the television on in Peanut's room, and Mama was by the front door on her cell phone talking to our cousin about the trip. T-Mobile didn't have good service in the woods, so the closer you were to the door or window, the better service you'd get.

About an hour later, we heard the house phone ring. No one answered the phone the first time, because we figured the caller had mistakenly called. But, when we heard the house phone ring again, I got out of bed to see who it was. I brought the phone to Mama, so she could answer it.

When she picked up, I walked back to my room, but she told me to come back, because the call was for me. I was shocked, because I didn't know who could possibly be calling me so late. For a second, I thought it was my biological mother, who must have gotten drunk, or that my friends were doing prank calls, but that wasn't the case. When I took the phone from Mama, a high-pitched, well-spoken, unfamiliar voice began to speak. The person ended up being my sister on my biological father's side. I was confused as to why she would call me suddenly; I had never heard of her or seen her a day in my life. Mama stood over me, listening, trying to figure out what was being said.

Moments later, tears of joy rolled down my cheeks. I didn't know if I should be a wimp and continue to cry or be a man and suck the tears in. My sister said, "Jacari, the family got together, and we decided to give you a call to know if you wanted to meet your father."

I shouted, "Yes! Of course, I would like to meet him."

What I didn't know was that I would be meeting him in the intensive care unit at Tallahassee Memorial Hospital. She informed me that he had been there for a few days now, and they thought it was best for me to see him. I promised her that I would stop by in the morning before we left. I couldn't be there for too long, because we were headed out of town. Mama was upset, not because they reached out but the way they reached out to me. She believed that they'd only contacted me because something was wrong with him, and they would have felt bad if I didn't meet him. Whatever their reasoning, I didn't care at the time. I was just happy that I had the opportunity to meet my father.

I went back to my bed to go to sleep. It was hard for me to sleep knowing that I would meet the man I'd once pronounced dead. Now that I knew he was alive, I believed that I could change his mindset, so he would step up and be the father to me he never had been.

The next morning, I quickly got out of bed to put on my clothes to prepare to see my father and get on the road to Orlando. I could tell that Mama still felt some type of way, but she eventually got over it, because she knew the situation was bigger than the both of us. When we walked in the intensive care unit, we had to check in and wait for the front desk receptionist to call the family room to verify that we could join them. The receptionist pressed the buzzer to let us in. A lady met us outside of the family waiting room -as one of my sisters. I smiled and gave her a hug, so things wouldn't seem awkward. Mama introduced herself and then we sat with the remainder of the family.

There was a waiting list to see my father, so Mama and I signed up and waited our turn. While waiting, everyone in the room was questioning me about what I was doing in life and about my future. They tried to connect the dots to see where I came along in the family and realized I was his last child. I didn't trust them, and I know Mama didn't either. They seemed to be moving a bit fast and expected quick answers to all the questions they were asking.

An hour passed by, and we were still waiting. Mama whispered and asked if she should tell the family that we were under time constraints, because we had to leave for Orlando in the next hour or we would miss our cruise. I told her she could with the hopes that they would understand. When she did, my sister who'd met us at the door told us that she would bump us up on the list so we could go inside. About fifteen minutes later, we were called back to room one fifty-seven. As I entered the room, I heard nothing, but the sounds of the machines attached to him. His room was dark, with no windows to let in the light. His face looked swollen. I could tell he was tall--perhaps taller than I was at the time--dark skinned, and much older than I'd thought he'd be, especially since I was a teenager.

I hadn't prepared myself to say anything; I didn't know where to start. The fact that I couldn't remember seeing him before this day only made it worse, so I just stood over his left side, looking at the cords connected to him and reading his monitors. He didn't know who I was until his wife told him. He looked at me and put his left hand out. I put my hand in his. I didn't know why he wanted to hold my hand, but I just did it, so I wouldn't seem disrespectful. While holding his hand, I kept wondering what he was thinking. If I took an educated guess, I believe he was wondering how I'd found him after all these years, the same question I wanted to ask my sister who'd called my house. Nevertheless, I continued to stand by him with my hand in his, wondering when he would let me go.

The doctor and nurses started coming in and out of the room to assess him. The doctor asked, "How are you related to him?" Before I could answer the question, the doctor went on and told me that I was a "strong man."

I smirked and said, "Thank you." The doctor and nurse continued their assignment, so they could leave the room. Mama sat in the corner, listening and watching everyone.

When they all left the room, it suddenly hit me that I was in the same room as my father. Despite his not being there for me, I wanted to do something for him. So, I asked everyone that came into the room to join hands, so I could say a word of prayer. Mama had always shared Bible stories with Peanut and I growing up, and one was about the woman who had an issue with her blood: Matthew 9:20-22. This sick woman had been praying for years to be healed from her sickness, until she learned that Jesus was coming to her city. She decided to walk up to him and touch his garment, and she was declared healed just in doing so. I figured that if two or three would join hands, I could pray his sickness away, so he could get better. I knew I wasn't Jesus, but I had a little oil in me after going to church a lot. I hoped once he was released from the hospital and off bed rest, he'd spend time with me. My prayer was short, sweet, and right to the point. I asked the Lord to heal him from the crown of his head to the soles of his feet. There wasn't much more I could do, or wanted to do, because he wasn't a real figure in my life.

Mama nodded her head toward the door as a signal that it was time to leave, so we said our farewells and left the hospital room. As we approached the family room, they asked if we could sit back down with them and talk over some information. I knew Mama was ready to go, and so was I. She told them we had to leave since we were in a rush, but we'd make sure to connect once we returned. The look on their faces read confused, disheartened, and shocked, but we weren't bothered by them, because I had done what I came to do—pay my respects. Anything else could be saved for later. Furthermore, we had a cruise ship to board. There was no need for me to be upset or look sorrowful, especially with us heading to a cruise to celebrate my birthday.

On the cruise, I made sure to do everything. I played morning bingo, went to the internet café and art shows, played mini golf, went to the spa and fitness room, did karaoke with my cousin until two o'clock in the morning, and I even snuck into the casino to play games I didn't know anything about except that there was a possibility that I could win money. I also ate as much as possible because the food was there, and because I could eat as much as I wanted.

As soon as we docked back at Port Canaveral, notifications started showing up on my phone. I hadn't had service for five days, and we couldn't afford Wi-Fi on the cruise. The voicemail that got my attention was from my father's wife. She requested for me to call her back when I got back on land.

I didn't know whether to call her as I was leaving the ship or if I should wait until we made it to Tallahassee. I asked Mama, and she advised me to call her back as soon as we had packed everything in the car. Once we were done, I gave my father's wife a call. I was going to hang up after the third ring, but Mama told me to leave a voicemail if she didn't pick up, so she couldn't say that I hadn't contacted her back. But she answered. As we talked, she shared some great news on my father's health. He was doing much better and had been moved out of the ICU and into a regular room. He would soon be discharged. I told her that when I arrived in Tallahassee, I'd give her another call to see if he was out, and if he wasn't, I was going to see him. She agreed, only if he was still going to be in the hospital—but she sounded as if she knew he'd be getting out that day.

Mama wanted to make a few stops to pay respects to the families who hadn't been able to come on the cruise due to financial issues or who couldn't take off from their jobs, so we went to their homes in St. Petersburg, Tampa, and Clearwater. When we arrived back in Tallahassee, Mama took Peanut back to town with Aymin, then we went home, unpacked our luggage and did laundry. Mama reminded me to call my father's wife, which I did, and she asked if we could meet them the upcoming Saturday. We stayed a far distance from each other, so we agreed to meet outside of a Burlington Coat Factory at eleven a.m.

On Saturday, Mama took me to breakfast first. She didn't believe in letting her children go anywhere without eating. Afterwards, we went to Burlington Coat Factory. We didn't know what type of car they had, so we decided to park in the No Parking zone, so he could see us when driving by. Twenty minutes passed, and we didn't see them, so Mama told me to text them, hoping that they would respond. A few moments later, he responded and told me that he would be pulling up in an old truck. We saw many trucks, but none of them were his, so I became upset. Mama had the heat on in the car since it was cold outside, but she started complaining that she was losing gas. Seconds later, an old truck rode beside us and parked. Mama and I didn't know if it was him through the truck's tinted windows, so I called him. It was, in fact, him. His wife wasn't with him.

As I left Mama's van, she told me to call her when I was ready, so she could pick me back up. That shocked me because Mama wouldn't normally leave me with strangers, but I saw the trust and excitement in her eyes.

When I got closer to my father's truck, I knocked on his driver's side window. He had a hard time letting it down, so he just stopped it halfway. He asked me how I was doing and told me how I had grown up to be a nice-looking young man, which made me smile and tell him the same thing. I went around the truck and got in on the driver's side. We chatted for a while, until he informed me that he couldn't walk around the mall due to his bad knees. He wasn't even able to get out of his truck, because he'd have a hard time getting back in. I was upset and disappointed because his wife had made it seem as if he would spend quality time with me, but that wasn't the case. All he wanted to do was see my face outside the hospital. I wanted to ask him why I hadn't heard from him in all those years, but he was already stumbling over his words, and I didn't want him to say anything that he wouldn't have meant to say. I left that subject alone. We talked for about ten more minutes, and then he told me he had to leave. I wasn't ready to go. I wanted to continue, but that didn't happen.

I called Mama to turn around and pick me up. By listening to her voice, I could tell she was angry. I knew she wanted me to spend more time with him, since he was never in my life. When Mama pulled up, we said our farewells and tears started rolling down my face. I felt played. I was his last child, and he didn't think to spend more time with me. I couldn't even get a full thirty minutes out of him. I knew that he didn't care; he had never really cared for me.

Mama told me that it would be okay, and that God does things for a reason. I never knew the reason, but whatever it could have been, it was over when he drove off. All I could see was a trail of smoke coming from his exhaust pipe. On our way back home, we went to the Southside Cemetery to visit the graves of family members who had passed away. We swept their graves with an old broom and put some flowers on their graves. Further down, there were three workers clearing the land, so they could have room to bury other people when they died. We left and went back home.

I haven't seen my father alive since that day. I called and talked to him a few times when he answered but didn't see him in person until he was lying in a casket at Strong and Jones Funeral Home six months later. The man that I had just met, the man who'd helped create me, the man who hadn't taught me anything about being a man was cold and empty. He was dead.

When I received the call about his death from my biological mother, I felt stuck and shocked. I didn't know how to tell Mama, because she was right when she'd told me that he'd only reached out because something was happening to him. Instead of keeping the news to myself, I politely knocked on her door and told her that my father had passed away. She was just as shocked as I was, because we didn't have all the details on his health, and we didn't expect his death to occur so soon, especially after recently meeting him.

At his wake, I stood over him and looked at all the makeup and detailing that the morticians had done. He looked very nice, suited with a pleasant smile. I shed a few tears and prayed over his body because I knew I wouldn't have that sacred opportunity at his funeral the following Saturday. After that, I was emotional and angry. I couldn't believe the person who helped me into this world had left the world right after

I met him. I had so many questions and built-up tears. I wasn't crying because he had died; I was crying because my own father hadn't taken the time to be with me or get to know me. No one was blocking the opportunity but him.

It was hard enough for me to know he was dead and that there would be no more opportunities for quality time, but to think of the many times my peers would laugh at me the day I told them I had finally seen my biological father hurt like hell. I knew they were only laughing because they were accustomed to having their fathers around, so they didn't know how it felt not having one. Mama and my biological sisters calmed me down and told me to read his obituary that was printed in the Thursday newspaper before his funeral. I tried to think of the positive things and the legacy that my father had left. After reading his obituary, it seemed as if everyone knew him except me. It stated that he was well-known in his community, was loved by many, and would be missed by all. I didn't think I was included in the "all;" I didn't have him in my life the way I deserved to. At that point, I was bitter.

EAGLE WINGS

The Friday before my father's funeral, I attended a family fish fry at his house. I felt awkward around my "family," because I had never met most of them, or I'd only met them once at the hospital. My other brothers and sisters, the ones my father had with my biological mother, were there as well, getting to know everyone and eating. I didn't want to seem ungrateful, but I wanted my fish to be fried hard, so I put in a special request to the fryer. He looked at me as if I shouldn't have asked then said, "Well, who are you?" I told him I was Charles's son. "Well, that's my daddy, too, and I never heard of you," he said.

I felt embarrassed but laughed it off, so it wouldn't seem as if I was being rude since he was much older than me and used his words back at him. "I never heard of you, either." On the inside, I was aggravated and ready to leave, because I felt disrespected, but I had to remember I came to pay respect to my father.

The fish was going to take a few extra minutes to fry, so he asked me to wait and gave me his number, so we could talk after the funeral. I didn't care too much to sit down with him, but he looked old enough to me to be my father, so I went on and followed his word. When my fish was finally done, I sat down on the front porch to eat. On the porch with me were younger family members who had heard about me and were glad to have me. I learned then that they were my nieces and nephews. We started talking about how close we were in age, the school we went to, and the extracurricular activities that we were involved in. At first, I wasn't going to share with them, because I didn't trust them, but they seemed genuine, and we ended up having a great conversation. We bonded well; it seemed as if we had known each other for years.

Before leaving the family fish fry, we traded numbers, promising to stay in contact with each other after the funeral. Afterwards, I left to go back home to prepare for the funeral that was happening the next day. Mama promised to make string beans with potatoes, and I planned to make my famous Seven Up pound cake for the repast. My brother and sisters on my biological mother's side, who had the same father as me, called and we spoke about the fish fry, deciding we would all walk into the funeral together.

The next morning, Saturday, the sun was shining bright, and a fresh breeze came through the windows in the living room while I was getting dressed. Mama didn't know what to wear, so she would throw on a dress or suit then come out to the living room and ask me which one she should wear. All her choices were nice, but I told her to go with the all-black dress, since I was wearing an all-black suit. After she got dressed, I quickly helped her put on her pearl necklace and earrings, since it was getting hard for her to do it by herself. Then we left to meet with the family at my father's house. Peanut didn't come; he wasn't re-lated to my father. We were joined together by my mother's blood only, and when I asked for him to come, his facial expression made it obvious that I shouldn't have even asked. The line-up for the family limousines started at ten a.m. When we arrived, cars were lined up all down the road and in the grass.

We found a parking space the next street over, and Mama started rushing me because it was getting late and she knew I'd have to leave soon with the family. At the house, everyone seemed happy; people were laughing and smiling like it was a family reunion. Mama and I just went with the flow.

When it was finally time to head to the church, I didn't think it was right for me to ride in the family limousines, because, though I was family, I didn't know anyone. I decided to get in Mama's car, so we could drive there together. When we turned the corner to get in the line of cars, the same sister who'd given me a call about seeing my father in the hospital tapped my window and told me that all his children had a seat in the funeral home limousine. I was hesitant to get out of the car. I didn't like being the black sheep, however Mama told me to go ahead and that she'd follow behind. In the car, they were sharing some great stories about "our" father, but the only stories I had of him was praying over him in the hospital and meeting him outside Burlington Coat Factory in the cold. No one had any more stories to share, and the driver hadn't left yet, because they were still trying to line the cars up correctly.

When everyone was lined up, the funeral director asked for the immediate family to get out of the limousines, so we could pray. Before the prayer, he gave reflections of his encounters with my father as they were good friends. If the look on my face didn't tell people how I felt about the stories they had of my father, I don't know what else would.

We finally got in our cars and headed to the church. Other drivers paid their respects to the funeral procession by pulling over to the side of the road as we drove by. When we arrived at the church, hundreds of people were in all black, standing in line by the entrance to the sanctuary, waiting to be seated. I stayed close with my sisters and we held hands two by two.

While in line, the funeral home director encouraged everyone to think of nice things my father had done in his life. I figured he was telling us that so we wouldn't be acting a fool as everyone walked by his open casket. I was fine. I couldn't think of anything else to cry about or be upset about, because I never knew him, and he had never impacted me. The line started moving, and my sister and I were up next. She squeezed my hand as soon as we stepped up to the casket. Moments later, while standing at the casket, tears started rolling down my face. They wouldn't stop, and I cried more and more. My sister and I were holding each other. The pain felt raw like an open wound. I couldn't understand what I was going through. Churchgoers came to get my sister and I and walk us to our seats. I was holding my stomach, stumbling to my seat. Before I sat down, Mama was there at the end of the row with her hands out wide, ready to hold and comfort me. It reminded me of how precious Jesus is to each of us. When we go through obstacles in life, his arms are extended to comfort us and let us know that everything will be alright.

When I read my father's funeral program, I became bothered, because the name that was printed in the obituary was not the name that I identified myself by. They'd called me "Jacari Williams," my name before I got adopted. I didn't appreciate that, and I felt disrespected, because I am a Harris boy; if they wanted to use any name, they should have used the name that I was given the day my adoption was finalized. My father wasn't there for my birth nor did he want to take me in, so why should I allow them to pick and choose when they wanted to claim me? Did they think I was dumb? He'd had only one job that day in the courtroom, and that one job was to step up and be a father to his children who were motherless and fatherless according to the Department of Children and Families.

I elbowed my sister, Kayla, so she could see what they had done. She, too, was in disbelief, because when she got adopted, her foster mother changed her last name as well. I continued reading through the program as they were giving the resolutions to the family, and I realized that my favorite homegoing poem that I'd requested to be inserted in the program was printed. I was happy but shocked that they'd heeded my request.

The poem, *I'm Free*, is one that I will cherish for years to come. Although I am not dead and don't have plans to die anytime soon, it allows me to believe that I was liberated from my biological family to be with a new family, one led by God. A portion of the poem reads:

> "Don't grieve for me, for now I'm free,
> I'm following the path God laid for me.
> I took his hand when I heard His call,
> I turned my back and left it all.

I felt great they'd included it, although I didn't really feel a part of the family. Throughout the program, I became more content, realizing that from the beginning of time, God had already planned out my life. He knew all about me before I was born. He knew what I would go through and how I would turn out. I finally stopped questioning Him; I knew that everything would be worked out in my favor.

After the funeral, we went to the burial site. As we approached the plot that my father would be laid to rest in, Mama reminded me that it was the same area that we had come to just a few months before when the workers were clearing the land, the day I met my father at Burlington Coat Factory. Who knew we'd be burying him there just a short time later?

When the gravesite services concluded, we went back to the church for the repast, where we all laughed and bonded. The homemade Seven Up cake I'd baked was gone as soon as I cut the first slice.

After my "family" apologized for not bringing me into the picture earlier, I learned that my father was a hardworking man who would work from dawn to dusk. He'd do anything to make ends meet. He was the doorkeeper at his home church and was respected within his community. I was happy to know we had similar characteristics when it came to getting work done, impacting lives, and leaving a legacy. On the inside, I was still upset. Everything looked good and sounded good, but it didn't feel good. No reason could explain why he didn't take the time to care and look after me, especially since I was his last child. Some people believed that I should get over it and be grateful that I was able to meet him before he died. Although I was grateful, that didn't close the gap. Instead, it left me with questions like, "Did he not love me enough?" Everyone wants to know that they're loved, especially vulnerable children.

As the sun started to set, Mama mentioned that it was about time for us to leave. Everyone promised to stay in contact with me, and I promised the same thing, only if they were willing to put in the time. To this day, I've never really tried to stay in contact with family members on my biological father's side. Most times, if I see one of them post a status or picture on Facebook, I'd comment under it and tell them how much I miss them, when I don't have anything to miss. I figured that it would make them feel good, but after a while I just stopped trying. We are all grown, have our own lives—I didn't think there was a need to add pressure on anyone I barely knew.

The week after the funeral, all hell broke loose. There was no will left behind. Everyone believed that they were entitled to my father's inheritance and property. I started receiving calls from both sides of my biological family. Everyone seemed to have questions, and others tried to ridicule me because I was the youngest child, so they believed that I wanted his money; I only wanted his love, something they were accustomed to, not me. My biological mother made it worse. She stayed on the phone calling all her children and my father's family, informing them that "Charles didn't do nothing for his children while he was living, so the least they could do is give his truck away, and allow Jacari to get his check until he turns eighteen." She was convinced that because I was his child that he owed me the world. My world had already shattered when I got the call about his death. There wasn't much more for me to do besides move on, just as I told everyone else to do. Don't get me wrong, the thought of getting free money sounded good, but Mama knew that wasn't going to happen since the adoption had already occurred. If I was eligible to get a check, I would have given it right to Mama, because I knew she lived paycheck to paycheck and that we were barely getting by. Yet, she was persistent, and we worked with what we had.

As the days went by, I realized I needed to get myself together. I wasn't happy with life and my biological mother's drinking habits got worse. I wanted to get my emotional and mental state together so that I could lead others in the right direction. This thought reminded me of Mama; how she had always been my backbone since she took me into her loving home. It wasn't her fault that I was in this situation, she wanted to make my life better regardless of the turmoil that was endured throughout the process. She was a natural born leader, and though she made a few mistakes, her goal was to guide her children so that they could be ready for the real world… and to take care of her. For this, I owe her hard work and dedication. I owe her my life.

THE NURSERY

A t the age of thirteen, I stayed home most of the time to help Mama care for the other foster children while she was busy at work. When I was free from babysitting, I would go outside and pick pears. One pear tree was adjacent to my bedroom window; the other was farther off. The biggest and sweetest pears were at the top, so I had to use a step stool to reach the fruit. Usually I had one of the other foster children outside with me to gather the pears as they fell. Hundreds of pears would fall, plenty to share with friends and family. If we had any leftovers, we would make pear doobie for dessert the upcoming Sunday.

One of the deacons was always the first to come over after church to get his bag of pears. Each time, he'd tell me, "I know you young, but if you want a few dollars in your pocket, stop by my house." I looked at him, then at Mama and smiled. I asked Mama if I could go, and she nodded. We passed his house every day, so I knew he had money; his house was two stories and sat on acres of land.

When he initially asked me to work for him, I didn't know what I would be doing. I thought maybe I would sweep his driveway or paint a room in his house, but no! He wanted me to work in the scorching-hot sun. He had multiple businesses, all of which required working outside. He had a carpentry business, where he sold swing sets, patio furniture, and rocking chairs. He had a wood business, where he sold firewood.

Over the summer he had a fresh produce business, with different kinds of fruits and vegetables from his garden.

My first day, I chopped and stored it in a shed, so he'd have excess during the rush season. My mind was focused on getting paid and going home. I was over it. Every time I rolled over wood; I saw bugs. Centipedes, caterpillars, roaches, ants, rollie pollies, and grasshoppers. Sometimes, I'd even see snakeskin. I gave up and asked if there was something else for me to do. When he saw that I wasn't making any progress, he told me I could come back after winter to help him start his garden. So, that's just what I did.

As soon as Christmas was over, I ran to his house and knocked on his door excited about helping him get his garden together. He told me to come back in about two weeks, and we would go over my schedule and pay. I smiled hard because anything with money sounded good, at least that is what I thought.

I wanted to be prepared, so I told Mama we needed to have a garden. She laughed and asked, "Will you be able to keep it up, because it's a lot of work, you know?" I told her yes, and we began the process of creating one.

The next day, I started looking for the right location. I figured that the open lot outside my bedroom window would be the best spot, because there was direct sunlight over it. Plus, I could see it from my window.

That weekend, Mama and I went to Lowes, Home Depot, Walmart, and a garden shop near her job so we could get everything. We planned to start working on the garden immediately after church, but I knew that the harvest would be bigger and better if I started that same day. I called my cousin who owned a tiller to help get the foundation started, so we could sow the seeds. After tilling the ground, I watered the dirt for a week straight then began integrating the fertilizer and planting.

Every morning before sunrise, I watered the garden and picked the weeds, because I was expecting a transformation to occur in the upcoming days. Before the sun went down, I prayed over the garden and watered it once more. I was so into the process of growing the garden that throughout the night, I'd get paranoid and think that someone was tampering with my garden, because I could hear all kinds of noises coming from outside. After a while, I finally began to see stems with tiny leaves coming out of the ground. Some seeds took longer than others, but eventually the entire garden was green. Mama often helped to ensure that each row was kept neat and that the walkway was free from weeds.

I continued watering the garden until it was harvest time. Soon, there wasn't one day that I wasn't harvesting vegetables. We had a garden full of collard greens, mustard greens, squash, cucumbers, tomatoes, onions, watermelon, sweet potatoes, okra and corn. The tomatoes, okra, and corn were the most challenging. The tomato stems started leaning, so I had to install wooden posts to keep them upright. I didn't know when it was the right time to pick the okra, so some were long and hard while others were medium. The corn took more work to grow; the plants were tall and took up a lot of space, and the racoons and crows would eat it every chance they got. Anytime I saw a racoon or crow near my garden, I would chase it away. I was happy to see the results from the seeds I had sown.

When it was time to start back working with the deacon, he had already started clearing this land where his garden would be. Right away, I started tilling the ground to break up the crusted soil and loosen up areas for planting. The deacon placed water sprinklers around the garden so we could make sure that every inch of the soil would get wet. Doing this helped plants move nutrients from the soil up through its stems and leaves. About two weeks later, it was time to start planting the vegetables and fruit—the planting process took two-three days to complete on his large plot. We got drained from the heat, and with his other small businesses, he had other duties to take care of that took up most of the day. Once everything was planted, he tasked me with pulling the weeds that grew throughout the season and watering the garden in the evenings. Eventually, we started seeing the fruit of our labor. Day after day, week after week, the beautiful plants grew strong and tall. The fragrance from the garden was like the sweet aroma of honeysuckle.

Knowing where we'd started—it was remarkable to see how this unused land had now become a beautiful, rich, green scene that passerby would admire from the road; it reminded me of a story from the Bible that Mama would always tell me. Jesus used stories to teach people many things about themselves and the world. In this story, Jesus spoke about a farmer sowing seeds. Some of the seeds had fallen into places where enough growth was impossible. Some fell by an old road, but the birds came and ate those seeds. Some of the seeds fell on unstable ground that didn't have enough dirt. Though the seeds grew, the plants died because the roots were not deep enough; other seeds fell in many thorny bushes and weeds, which ultimately stopped the plant from growing.

I knew where she was headed by telling me this story. She wanted me to understand that I couldn't just sow seeds anywhere, and she wasn't just speaking about the garden. She was speaking about the seeds that I would have to sow in life. For me to have a bountiful harvest, I needed to listen to the voice of God, and sow seeds that would take me further than I could ever imagine. The same seeds that I sowed in the physical garden had to be sown with the understanding that good care, and patience would result in the best reward. To have a bountiful harvest as it relates to my personal and professional goals and the seeds, I sow for them, I must also take good care of myself and have patience.

SECOND COMES AFTER FIRST

A fter sixth-grade, Mama decided to move me to another middle school. She realized that I wasn't adapting to the charter school, which was only going to lead me to more trouble. I ended up going to the school closer to home, a public school by the name of Montford Middle. I started opening and growing mentally, physically, spiritually, and emotionally, competing in cross country and track at the school and playing football and basketball for the city of Tallahassee. I was a linebacker on the field, a beast on the court, and a snail on the track. During those days, I felt rejuvenated and started to really see myself for who I was. I started to become more active in my community and within my school, trying to overcome any obstacle in my way. I tried my best to get lost in building my craft rather than reminiscing over what I had been through. Though, sometimes, despite my best efforts, I went back to my old ways of acting out. For the most part, though, I was becoming a new person. I entered many school competitions and educational programs that would enhance my academic skills. My favorite club was the Black History Brain Bowl team. I wasn't into learning much about the black culture and history until I joined. At that point, I began investigating issues that many people of African descent faced before and during my time.

Even though I didn't start my educational career off on the best path, by the conclusion of my middle school days, I felt better about myself. I started smiling more and having more positive experiences. I knew that the next phase of my life would be high school, so I began to prepare for what was to come. Peanut was already in high school, but he wasn't doing so well with his academics. He was too busy worrying about the next party or when the latest Jordan's would come out. Or, he was trying to be like his friends and stay on cloud nine. Not saying that there is anything wrong with having fun with your peers or knowing when the latest styles are released, but those things couldn't give him a high school diploma. Mama always taught us that education is the foundation of success. Growing up, she would tell us, "Go to school, get your lesson, do your work, so when you get older, you'll be able to have a job." What she was trying to tell us was that if we got some sort of degree behind our names, people would respect us more and give us a decent wage.

The trail of the mighty Trojans set me free. The day I stepped on the grounds of Lincoln High; I didn't know what to expect. I was overwhelmed with the expectations of others and myself. People told me that I needed to "get all A's," and "attend every class," so I could be categorized as an Honor Student or given award for the best attendance. All I wanted to do was get a diploma. I didn't care about anything else. In fact, I didn't care about the diploma as much, either. It was a piece of paper. With the advancement of technology and resources, I was sure that I could learn everything I needed to on my own while using books and online resources. At the time, I would have rather done that than to sit in a class listening to a teacher lecture for most of the day.

During high school orientation, I thought I was at a university. There were thousands of people squirming around, trying to meet their prospective teachers. I couldn't grasp the concept of how I could walk to my classes with other students crowded around me. I couldn't even stand in comfort. How would I be able to eat in a timely manner with all these students? So many questions pushed to my mind. I was worried and afraid. A dark-skinned lady with a short hairstyle noticed how lost Mama and I were. We were both looking at the campus map displayed on a board, trying to find my English I class. She came over with another student who was in a wheelchair. Immediately, she realized where we were trying to go and told us to follow her lead. A few minutes later, we were at the door of the English I course. We thanked her for helping us, and she went inside the next door. After we were done meeting all my teachers, we left the grounds of the campus and went shopping.

Though parents were mostly excited about taking their children back to school after summer break, going shopping for school clothes was my most-favorite part. We'd go during tax-free weekend, the week before school started. For my first years in high school, Mama set the budget at four hundred dollars for each of us to get all the clothes and shoes we wanted for the semester. After shopping with Mama several times before, I knew how to shop and catch deals. Even though I spent all my money, I had the most clothes and shoes out of all of us.

After starting classes, I noticed how unhappy I was about some of the students in my courses. Some, I knew from elementary and middle school, some from church, but the others I didn't know. The ones that I didn't know were looking at my clothes and shoes and laughing, but I just knew I was looking good, because it was the first week of class—the week everyone, myself included, wore their best outfits. Almost everyone had new clothes, so I knew it wasn't my clothes they were laughing at. I figured they were laughing at the way I was walking or talking as I entered the room. I was walking swiftly, and my voice was raspy since I was going through puberty.

I wasn't accustomed to large campuses and lost my way trying to find my first class. I didn't want to be the student that was late on the first day, but after finding out that I was in the wrong building, I had no choice but to accept my fate.

When I did finally find my class, I gazed through the classroom door, and all eyes were looking my way. I was spooked. I didn't know what my next move should be, so I just stood at the entrance, waiting to be directed by the teacher. Ms. Talley was a younger Caucasian woman with dyed black hair and a nice smile. She was still taking roll when I entered the room. When she got to my name, she looked at me because I was the only one standing and the last name on the roster. Finally, she assigned me to my seat in the corner by people I didn't know. I remained focused, knowing that I was not in school to have friends but to leave in four years with a piece of paper as my confirmation that I'd completed all the necessary courses to graduate.

The student who was sitting next to me was picking his nose. I was disgusted and rolled my eyes then looked the other way. When I turned back around, he continued to stare at me, which bothered me. No matter where I moved, his eyes followed me. Day after day, he continued to stare. I didn't see him any other time throughout the day except lunch, because we didn't have any other classes together.

One day, I asked to go to the bathroom just to see what he'd do. On my way back to class, there he was, at the water fountain, smiling and looking right at me as if I owed him something. I was getting pissed; it seemed as if I was being stalked. I only wanted to know what his issue was. If I had the chance, I would have given him a piece of my fist. Walking back toward class, I started having flashbacks of the days that I was followed by the Department of Children and Families when having visitation with my biological mother. We never really had privacy in those situations, and the dude who was following me and looking at me wherever I went obviously didn't know what privacy was. To calm myself down, I got some water, went back to class, and sat down quietly to finish completing the assignment for that day.

The third week into the academic year, I got suspended for an entire week because of that guy. He filed a complaint about me with the

Dean of Students' office, stating that I'd shoved him in the hallway on the way to the class—which I had, because I got tired of him following me. When Mama got the call to come pick me up for my suspension, she was livid. I not only had my phone taken away, but I couldn't go to choir practice or even to my best friend's birthday party. The entire week I was suspended, I had to clean the house and rake the yard. Mama wanted her house spotless and her yard leaf-free.

When I returned from my suspension, the entire school knew what had occurred. I did my best to stay distant from the issue, but my peers continued to question me, curious to know why I had pushed the boy. Before I could get to my Earth Space Science class, I was called into the office of Student Affairs.

"Now what have I done?" I asked myself.

As I walked into the office, there were three people there: the principal, the school deputy, and the kid who I had pushed. As soon as I realized the point the administration was trying to make, I started smirking. They wanted me to apologize to the boy when it was essentially his fault that everything had occurred.

"Stupid people," I whispered under my breath.

I sat and listened to the ongoing lecture about being nice to my peers and the effects of bullying. The fact that the administration was calling me a bully bothered me. Once more, I was defined as something that wasn't really me. I immediately left without permission, for I knew had I not, I would have been expelled from the school for my relentless mouth.

Seconds later, I heard my name over the intercom informing me to report to In School Suspension (ISS). I wasn't too upset, because I had been in ISS plenty of times in middle school.

I sat in this suspension room all morning, looking at the four walls, doing nothing. I was boiling on the inside. I began tapping my right foot on the floor to aggravate the assistant vice president. He became very annoyed and told me, "Your next step is to be removed from this school." I stopped tapping my foot, and shortly after it was time for lunch. During lunch break, I thought I would be able to leave to get something to eat, but the food was brought to me in ISS. I stayed there in the same seat for the remainder of the day, trying to find any excuse to leave, but nothing worked.

When I got home, Mama informed me that she'd received a call about my time in ISS. She told me it was best for me to "shut-up and listen to folks." I thought she was trying to be funny, because we all knew the school administration was full of funny people, but this was no joke. She wanted me to get my act together, so I could have a successful high school journey.

The next morning, I had to report back to ISS and was given my package of work that my teachers had put together, so I wouldn't get behind on my work from the week of suspension and now ISS. I completed an entire week worth of class work, homework, and tests in about four hours. If I had a choice, I would have preferred to complete a week worth of work in one day, so I could do what I wanted to do with the other time that I had, but I knew that once I got out of ISS, that option wouldn't be available.

After lunch, I was bored. I couldn't go to sleep, and I couldn't get on my phone since it was confiscated that morning. So, I started writing. I'm not sure why, I don't know how I came up with the idea to write, especially because I hated taking intensive reading, but it kept me busy and focused.

My name is Jacari Etienne Williams Harris, and I will do better.
My name is Jacari Etienne Williams Harris, and I will do better.
My name is Jacari Etienne Williams Harris, and I will do better.

I wrote this hundreds of times, nonstop, as if I had a story to tell, but I realized that I was telling it through my walk and talk. The more I wrote the same sentences over and over, the more I wanted to better myself, because all I had was my name, which was very valuable to me. Sometimes, we must see or go through the same things to understand the bigger picture.

As soon as I was released from ISS, I began to do my best to get on all my teachers' good sides. I was determined to be a better student. Though I had more behavioral issues later in my freshmen year, I was able to get promoted to the next grade level, so I could continue my journey to high school graduation.

The summer leading into my tenth-grade year, I started reading different genres of books. I would always read fiction works, as I love to read how authors piece together made-up stories. One of my favorites was The Adoration of Jenna Fox by Mary E. Pearson. Jenna was a young woman who was in a coma after a car accident who couldn't remember her life before the tragic accident. With her family and friends, she tried to discover who she really was, but she could not. Eventually, she believed that she was no longer her real self. The novel took me on a life-changing voyage through questions of bio-restorative morals and the idea of humankind.

From that point on, my perception about many things began to change drastically. I started wondering if I was being my real self. I couldn't find the answer, because my life was controlled by a system and my adopted family. My thoughts and actions began to transform into something bigger than myself.

When my report card finally came in, I was nervous. I didn't know what to expect. I wasn't the best reader and I hated math, so I was hanging on with a prayer. Mama always based our summer trips and plans off course grades. Thankfully, my grades were great, and Mama was pleased. She took her time to review the teacher's feedback. Typically, in high school teachers don't give feedback, however comments were left for my intensive reading course. These comments were: "Jacari displays a sense of urgency of learning new material, which encourages his classmates to study more outside of the classroom and be attentive during class lectures. Furthermore, Jacari tends to get upset if he doesn't get the desired grade he wishes for, but still puts in the work to ensure that his next assignment grade is to his liking. We're glad that Jacari is pushing himself to be better each day."

I didn't know how to feel because the feedback showed several sides of me all based on how I reacted to my own feelings and emotions. What stood out the most is that she believed in me, which allowed me to believe in myself. From then on, I felt as if I was able to conquer anything, because I had completed my freshman year of high school—something that seemed impossible to do at the beginning of the school year.

At the end of that school year, mid-summer, I set up a meeting with my guidance counselor, so I could begin to register and solidify my fall courses for sophomore year. The meeting didn't go so well. I was informed that I could not graduate high school on time, since I didn't pass the state-wide math exam that I'd taken earlier in the year. I felt doomed, but I was determined. Sadly, I had already been held back in the first grade due to immaturity, so I could not allow myself to fall behind another year.

The guidance counselor offered me the opportunity to take the state-wide exam before the first quarter in the semester was over, so I took the offer. I started proclaiming, "I will pass this exam, I will pass this exam," to myself to get myself psyched for it. To my surprise, I passed the exam. When I went back to my counselor and informed her of the results, she was shocked! In fact, she told me that I was one of very few who passed it on the second try.

It was now possible for me to graduate high school in three years instead of four, if I worked hard enough to stay ahead. That would make up for the year I was held back in elementary school. When I shared this with her, she told me that many of her former students who tried to catch up set themselves back by trying to take on too much. I felt defeated, but I didn't allow her to see that. Instead, I started making declarations about how I would make up for that year I was behind. I didn't know how or if it was even possible, but I was going to do my best to make it happen. I was disappointed by the lack of support from my peers and some of the faculty members, but I knew that I would make my dream a reality. They believed that I would get overwhelmed with all the added work and quit.

The next week, I went back to my guidance counselor with a plan, informing her of what I was going to do and how I was going to do it. I had already started the process of contacting people who I knew could help me achieve my goal, even if they didn't believe in it. I scheduled a meeting with all my teachers, the administrator for virtual courses, and the graduation staff. I already had bi-weekly meetings with my guidance counselor as we would both check-in with each other on the progress that I had made. I came up with an agenda and started making plans about my own destiny. From then on, I told myself that I wouldn't allow anyone to tell me what I could or could not do in my life.

The guidance counselor wasn't the only person who doubted me. My own adoptive mother did as well. It wasn't because she didn't want me to achieve my goals but because she allowed the guidance counselor to talk her into believing how challenging it would be to get it done. One of my classmates heard about my efforts to graduate on time and decided to join me on this journey since she had also been held back in elementary school. We encouraged each other and helped to keep each other sane. I started taking virtual courses—a total of seventeen additional courses over three academic semesters, while still being a full-time in-class student. Though it was tedious and overwhelming at times, I knew that my destiny would be greater. If I stood committed to the vision, nothing would be impossible.

As time went on, Mama was having a hard time making ends meet, so I decided to get a job to help. I got my first job at McDonalds at the age of sixteen. I didn't know that I would end up working for the same restaurant that I had visitations at with my siblings and biological mother when I was younger. I worked a minimum of thirty-five hours a week—sometimes more, depending on my school schedule. Most of the time, I would try to get overtime to make more money. It felt good to walk into the store and buy whatever I wanted. Even though I was a minor, I knew I would be breaking laws by working too many hours during a school week, but if the store didn't get caught by the corporate office, I'd be okay. To my surprise, we never got caught. None of the crew members or managers understood why I wanted to work so much, but I knew the plan I had for myself and that was all that mattered to me. I didn't have much of a social life, because I was determined to reach my goal.

Some nights, I would be clocked in at work until I was kicked off the clock. Peanut always told me that our biological mother did the same thing when trying to take care of all seven of us when we were under her care. Unfortunately, it never worked out for her, because she got overwhelmed. I knew it would work out for me. When I got home from work, I would take a shower and eat dinner. My dinner usually consisted of a free meal from McDonald's, so I was doing Mama a favor by not having to cook as much. I didn't miss one of those meals. I'd never imagined the opportunity to receive a free meal from one of my favorite fast food restaurants growing up. I couldn't resist the urge of going home with hot fries, extra salt, and chicken nuggets.

After eating dinner, I'd go right to bed. When I heard yelling, I knew it was Mama waking me up to get ready for school. Although I struggled to get up, thinking about all I needed to accomplish got me going. It wouldn't take me long to get dressed, because I'd wear my usual sweatpants, hoodie, and Nike slides. At the time, I didn't care what people thought of me. "Dressing like I didn't have any clothes" as Mama would say. I didn't learn until college that your image really matters to people. Not only to friends but to professionals as well. It takes no time for someone to judge you based on your looks, so, though I didn't care in high school, in college, I dressed for success. Besides, I had a lot on my plate to worry about what someone would think of me—I knew their thoughts would change when they would see me walk across the graduation stage the next academic year.

Before summer break, I had my last meeting with the guidance counselor. During this meeting she made the final decision on if I was on target with my graduation goal— I was. I knew her belief in my goals changed when I saw the big Kool-Aid smile on her face.

Who knew that the young, Black, misbehaved, and misunderstood child would learn the value in financial stability, the need to work hard to achieve, and the importance of looking the part? It took a lot of prayers, a long identity search, and dreams to get to this point. I'm nowhere near my peak, but I am well on my way.

Overcoming Doubt

T he sun was just rising, shining brightly through the hole in my window curtain. I could hear thumps of rain gliding down the side of the house and birds chirping through the chimney. I was stuck in the same position for an hour, frightened, trying to remember what I had dreamed about the night before. When I turned over on my left side, I realized that I was in a cold sweat.

I decided to take a hot shower and put on my favorite outfit, so I could go to school. This time, it was my red and black high-top Jordan's, with a South Pole shirt and black jeans.

Thirty minutes later, I was at school hearing the last bell ring, so I ran to class, trying not to be late. I had to make it to my civic engagement class before the daily quiz was handed out, so I wouldn't receive an automatic zero. I couldn't afford a zero, because it would take me at least five assignments to get my grade back up. Finally, I made it to class. The teacher was just giving the quiz to the last student in my row, so I was able to take it.

Class was dismissed immediately after submitting the quiz, so I headed to gym class. I didn't like this class, because I had to change in front of other boys. It was disturbing to think about the act of changing clothes in front of people I didn't know or trust. I was paranoid. I would wait until the locker room got down to one or two people before I undressed. While others were changing, I would concentrate on my cell phone, pretending as if I was receiving text messages from friends. The school didn't have internet service, and I had a Virgin Mobile phone, so there was no way to receive messages. But I pretended anyway.

One day, I patiently waited for everyone to change, and it seemed as if all the boys were laughing at me, since they knew I wouldn't change clothes in front of anyone. The coach came in and started yelling, "What's takin' you all so long? Females take longer to get dressed, not males." I started smirking and continued to play on my phone. Many of the students changed then left the room.

Even when the room cleared, I still surveyed my surroundings, making sure that no one else was able to see me. A few minutes later, a classmate came over and just stood there, watching me. I ran into the bathroom stall and he started laughing, but I didn't know why.

There was one male student who I began laying my eyes on. I couldn't say anything to him, and I couldn't act out of order because I didn't know if it was something I really wanted to do. We didn't have any classes together, but we both had great personalities, so when we had a chance, we would hang out together after school hours. While school was in session, I just did my normal school routine: go to class, walk the halls until security caught me. We started going to third period lunch together and became closer friends. But he never knew I was thinking of him in another context. I didn't want our friendship to end since I knew he wasn't into dating other boys too much conflict would arise between the mutual friends that we both shared. And, at that time, I didn't know if I was even into boys. I was fighting my feelings within, and I didn't want anyone to know that side of me. Well, at least I thought I didn't until I faced my fears later in high school.

I didn't want to burn any bridges with those around me, so I often just fantasized about the dudes I was interested in without telling anyone. At this point, I didn't know much about the true meaning of relationships, so I was only attracted to people superficially, based on their looks. Most of the times, the dudes I was looking at weren't even gay.

This time, it started in my messages on Facebook. Each day when I got home from school, I'd receive a message from someone who looked very familiar; I just couldn't catch on to where I knew them from. I knew he went to the same high school as me because his Facebook profile bio indicated that he went to Lincoln High School. While going to and from each class, I would pay close attention to every boy who spoke to me, stared at me, opened the door for me, just to see if I could get a clue of who it could possibly be.

After a few weeks of messaging each other, I realized I recognized him because he took the same bus that I did to school. In fact, he lived four bus stops away from me—less than two miles apart from his home to mine. I noticed his face this time, because he decided to sit across from me. Typically, a few students would ride the school bus in the morning, so I wasn't accustomed to someone sitting near me. Before we got off the bus to start the school day, we traded our cell numbers and started texting and speaking more. I started getting afraid that someone would pick up my phone and read my messages, so I decided not to text him anymore. Instead, I promised him that I would sit by him on the bus in the mornings as we headed to school.

I would wake up late and miss the bus on purpose or try to take another route to school, so I wouldn't see him. As much as I wanted to see him, I didn't understand what was going on with my feelings because they were everywhere. I was afraid to talk to my family about him because they didn't think I was interested in anyone outside of friendship, and I hadn't disclosed any information about my sexuality.

Unfortunately, I didn't know what "love" meant at that time, because I was overwhelmed by my biological and adopted families. Though my biological family said that they loved me, my adopted family showed it, so these were emotions I always struggled to understand. Now this just added another element to it. Although I didn't have a father figure in my life, I did the best that I could: groomed well, dressed well, and spoke well, trying to fit in with everyone else. A man was supposed to teach me how to be a man and show me how to get and treat a woman, but there was no one in my life to do that. I was finding my way on my own, and my own way led me to be interested in the same sex.

As time went on, I felt like I was being watched by my family and friends, so I barely said or did anything. I would still go to his house and hang out with him a couple hours after school. When Mama found out through my cousin that I was at someone else's house, she started questioning me on my whereabouts. I would always respond that I was studying and doing group projects with friends, but she knew better than to believe that. I don't blame her for asking questions about my whereabouts, because I wasn't making wise decisions on how I could still live how I wanted to live and not let others find out. I would get off the same bus stop as him, knowing good and well that people would be curious as to why I wasn't getting off at my bus stop.

I didn't talk to anyone about my feelings that I had towards him—or if I even really had any to begin with. I was hoping that they would go away, but it seemed as if the more I spent time with him the more I was digging myself into a hole that I couldn't get out of.

Weeks later, I opened to some of my close friends and cousins about my sexuality. My close friends (who were mostly girls) proclaimed they already knew. They also knew that I was afraid to speak on my feelings towards men, but they knew that when I was ready, I would have let them know. I had to be ready, because the hole I was digging seemed to keep getting deeper. If I didn't speak up when I did, I would have buried myself in my own beliefs that no one really knew that I was interested in other boys. I asked them not to tell anyone around the school. When I told my cousin, she laughed with amazement in her eyes because she, too, already knew that I was battling with my sexuality. She told me that she still loved me, and that she wanted me to be safe, be happy, and find love. She said I deserved to be loved the right way after going through so much growing up. I smiled with tears rolling down my face, because I had thought that if she wouldn't accept me for who I was, no one would. After sharing with her how my sexuality came about, I begged her to not say anything to anyone—especially my mom, because I knew that she wouldn't accept my new lifestyle.

I did my thing with whoever I decided to lay down with—just a handful. They expressed interest in me either by asking for my number to get help with homework—which soon led to them trying to have sex—or by them just stating that they were interested in me. Barely anyone close to me knew, unless I told them, or I got caught. I did all that I could and more, just so I could feel that someone loved me—only until I felt ashamed and stopped seeing guys for a while did I realize that it wasn't love; it was lust. At least, in the beginning of my experiences I thought it was all love, but now I know that having sex with different people isn't what love really is.

Mama oftentimes wondered what was going on with me. She never knew about my sexual activities at the time. She was too busy trying to figure out what other people thought about me rather than coming to me herself and asking. She would ask me if I was dating or why I didn't have a girlfriend yet like my brothers had. I knew she didn't like when men went the other way, so I would lie and tell her that a relationship wasn't my primary goal. She, however, eventually found out through a church member. Undoubtedly, the church member had seen me walking very close to a guy on the sidewalk. Although, I could have argued that I didn't believe walking closely to another dude on a sidewalk indicated that I was gay, I didn't have the energy to hide it anymore. My older brothers would tease me about even the possibility of me being gay and would laugh in my face, saying degrading comments like when Peanut told me, "God made Adam and Eve, not Adam and Steve."

I was hurt, because I knew I wasn't perfect, and I knew that I loved the Lord. It felt like I had everything together except for my sexuality, while others had their sexuality together but other components in their life were in shambles. You see, people can act as if they have it all together, but when they go to bed at night and can't go to sleep, or are waking up throughout the night because their imperfections are haunting them, they should think about how unqualified they are to degrade anyone else's imperfections.

As a Christian, my denomination was Primitive Baptist. In the church, the pastors don't preach about gay couples, because dating the same sex is sinful and "not of Christ," as the church folks will preach to you. Internally, I knew that being interested in the same sex wasn't the best decision, based on biblical philosophy, but it made me happy.

What really got under my skin was that many people talked badly about individuals who were interested in the same sex, as if there were no other sins. As a Christian, growing up in a Baptist church, I knew that the church members wouldn't accept my lifestyle, so I tried not to give hints about my being interested in men for fear they would condemn me. Soon, I stopped caring about what people had to say about me. No one was perfect no matter how hard they tried to be.

One day, on our way back from Bible study, a short, skinny, four-eyed, truck driver was at the same stoplight we were at. She knew Mama, so she would always speak when we saw her. This time, she waved her hand and signaled for Mama to roll down her window. They chatted quickly at the light, but she didn't neglect to mention to Mama that she thought I had a little "sugar in my tank." Mama looked at me in embarrassment and said that all her boys were interested in women. Mama already knew; she just didn't want others to know. I really didn't care what the woman thought of me, because by the way she dressed, she looked as if she was a man herself—so I always thought she was into women too. Anytime I saw her after that evening, I cut my eyes at her. I knew she was right; I just needed to act as if she wasn't, so she wouldn't go around and tell other people. I didn't want people in my personal business, especially if I could prevent it.

After a while, I just stopped talking to people of both genders. I was tired of folks judging me based on assumptions and hearsay. Though they were right about some of the stories they'd heard about me, I didn't want to acknowledge it. Some guys I was entertaining would slip up and tell their friends that they were "talking to me." And sometimes I would come off flamboyantly unintentionally. I would sometimes put my hands on my hips, constantly roll my eyes and do other feminine gestures that persuaded others that I was gay without me even having to say so. Soon, I realized there were other people living in secret too, and I was relieved.

Two of my biological sisters on my mother's side were into the same sex as well. I found out when we met up at Fun Station to ride on go-carts. They had invited their significant others and introduced them to me as their girlfriends. I was shocked for their braveness because I didn't know that they were into girls. Once they introduced me to their girlfriends, I decided to become transparent as well and tell them about my interest in boys--they proclaimed that they already knew by the way I was acting, and we all started laughing. After that, our relationships got stronger. We talked about everything under the sun, from the people we dated to school, work, and the childhood memories we could rekindle from before the separation.

Our conversations meant everything to me. I became more confident and started loving myself more. Then I got into my first relationship. It wasn't all that bad. I learned from it. A couple years later, I got into my second relationship, this time with a woman. I wanted to test the waters. We went on several dates, spent the night with each other, went to Jacksonville for the weekend, and did any and everything we wanted to do. She was a few years older than I was, but I was mature enough to understand what I was working with. Months later, I became too busy trying to live my best life before I graduated high school, so I wasn't concentrating on any relationship. I felt as if I had tested the waters enough. I'm sure I broke her heart, something I am not pleased with; however, I am grateful for everything she taught me, and the unforgettable experiences we had together.

Then came my friend Vickie. We'd started out as friends when we met in U.S. history class my sophomore year in high school. We grew so close that when it was time to register for courses the following semester, we tried our best to get into the same classes. We would go to lunch and explore the city together. There were times when I would give in to the feelings beyond friendship that I had for her and try to get into a relationship with her. But I realized I just didn't have those kinds of feelings for her, no matter how good of friends we were.

The day she demanded that I take her to our school's senior prom, I knew I had messed up. She even told everyone we were going together before I could agree. I had no choice but to go with her, because I didn't want to hurt her feelings. As prom season approached, many of our classmates were asking each other out to prom, and she expected for me to do the same thing. I didn't feel comfortable doing it, because she already knew that we were going. I also didn't want her to feel we were in a relationship—she refused to believe that we weren't. Furthermore, I wasn't the type to say or give corny things just to ask someone out on a date, especially if we weren't together. Some classmates planned an entire event just to ask their date to prom, others made cute cards, large signs with cut-outs, and gave flowers. I wasn't going to waste my money or time when I knew we were already going.

But after seeing so many of our friends asking each other to prom, I felt bad, so I told everyone that we were going together. Then I learned she was telling our peers that we were going to get married and have kids. I didn't know how to feel, because I wasn't ready for marriage. We were too young, not to mention, I was still figuring myself out.

By this time, prom was a week out, so we started making plans for our prom night. As her date, I did my best to execute her dream on a reasonable budget. During that time, I also reminded her that we were going to prom as good friends, nothing more, nothing less. She agreed, but her actions said differently. She wanted me to rent a limousine for the evening or get a rental car. We weren't qualified to rent a car. The legal age was twenty-five, and we had only recently turned eighteen. Secondly, our parents weren't going to go out of their way to rent a car for prom, so that was a no.

For dinner, she wanted us to go to the most expensive restaurant in town. I didn't know what she meant by "expensive," as I was accustomed to going to buffets with my family. Afterwards, she wanted to get a room at Hotel Duval in downtown Tallahassee. She also requested to have a personal photographer that would follow us throughout the entire day. I knew I couldn't afford everything she requested, but I would do what I could within my budget.

Despite it all, the day before prom, I hired a photographer. I asked Mama to borrow her new 2014 Kia Sorento. I didn't know what restaurant she wanted to go to, I stayed up all night on Google searching for top restaurants downtown. By the time I was ready to go to sleep, I had narrowed it down to Golden Corral or The Front Porch.

The morning of prom, I asked Mama to decide between the two restaurants, and she told me to take her to The Front Porch, as it was a better setting for a "date." After calling the restaurant and reserving a table for two, I got my hair cut, picked up the boutonniere, corsage, and two dozen purple roses. I took the roses to the restaurant, so the waitress could place them on our table before our arrival.

I got dressed in my all-white tuxedo, with a purple vest, a purple bowtie, and white shiny dress shoes. When Mama came back from getting the car washed, I left for Vickie's house to take pictures and head to prom. She had on a purple ball gown with jeweled scales centered around her chest. Her make-up was just right, hair curled the way I liked it—she looked beautiful. I put the corsage on her, and she put the boutonniere on me; then we were off to our prom events.

At dinner, we laughed and talked about our time in high school and what we looked forward to once we headed to Florida State University, the location where our prom was being held. After asking for the bill, I paid, and the waiter informed my date that the roses on the table belonged to her. Her expression was written all over her face, overjoyed.

While at prom, Vickie wanted me to dance with her, but I didn't know how to. But I tried my best and ate as much food as I could. When prom was over, she wasn't ready to go home. She wanted to go out with all our friends, but I wasn't up for it, because I had church in the morning.

Instead of going out, we both agreed to go to McDonald's to get some ice cream. We both worked there and wanted to also show off our attire for the evening. On our way, my phone constantly buzzed. She was upset that people were texting me throughout the evening, because she wanted my full attention. She tried to take my phone while I was driving, but I didn't let her. As we got out of the car, my phone fell from my lap and was stuck in between the driver seat and the center console. As I was trying to grip the phone, she grabbed it under the seat, and I attempted to get it back, but she wasn't having that. She started going through my messages. I immediately knew what messages she had read, because she started crying and yelling. I knew I had disappointed her, but had she not been nosy, she wouldn't have read the messages I'd been sending to the guys I was entertaining at the time. I truly didn't have the patience to deal with her, because nothing I said would change her mind. All I could think of was the fact that I'd tried to tell her that we weren't together. Now that she'd read those messages, I knew she would come to her senses.

I was wrong. After that incident, she started arguments with me day in and day out, during class and while on the clock at work. One day, she said she hoped for me to choke on my food and die. The next day, she tried to lure me into having sex with her by telling me her sexual desires and how I shouldn't be sexual with anyone except for her. Her controlling ways didn't sit well with me. We weren't in a relationship, and our friendship was diminishing. I wanted her to look at the bigger picture of what we could become—life-long friends—but her actions wouldn't allow that.

During the last two weeks of school, I had to find another way to walk to class, because she would start bugging me as soon as she saw me in the hallway. I started to believe that she purposely walked my route to class, so I could see that she was still upset, but when she walked by, she wouldn't even speak to me. In class, I decided to switch seats to be out of her way, but that never helped, because she was too obsessed and wanted revenge. She still wanted to know that she had my attention, so she would try to make me jealous by talking to other boys in class and rubbing on their legs. I thought it was funny, because she was making a fool of herself.

Our friendship fell apart. We couldn't work the same shifts anymore. The manager would send one or both of us home, because we weren't following the company's policies regarding issues with other employees. We were supposed to report to the store manager if we were being harassed, bullied, or having issues with other employees. I never reported her, because I knew it wasn't that serious. As issues continued to arise, my hours started getting cut, which was essentially messing with my money. I knew that she wanted me to feel the way she was feeling, but I couldn't feel that way because we were just friends.

The last time I talked to her was the day she asked to go to the movies, and I told her no. I didn't want her to think I was leading her on, so it was best for me to deny the invitation. Instead, I went to get a haircut, and afterwards, I went to McDonald's to get some ice cream. When ordering my ice cream at my job, the manager, who I was very cool with, told me that Vickie had been coming to McDonald's throughout the entire afternoon and evening, which was unlike her, because there was another McDonald's closer to her house. I knew it was time for me to go home before she came back up there, but I was a minute too late. While walking out of the exit, she pulled up like a bat out of hell and parked close to my car so that I could only get to the driver's side through the passenger door.

I side-stepped her car, hopped into my own, and backed up to leave, praying that she would go home too. She drove on my tail all the way to the exit of the parking lot. I made a quick left back into the main parking lot, and she started speeding to stay on my tail. I thought she was playing, but she chased me around the McDonald's building until I tried to flee home. I knew that Mama would have straightened her out had she followed me all the way home, but my car wasn't having it. The harder I pressed the gas pedal the more my car shook. I was nervous, sweating, and afraid that we would get hurt or killed. I called her friend to see if she could calm Vickie down, but that didn't work either. According to the best friend, Vickie wouldn't even listen to her.

She chased me around Walmart's parking lot until I was trapped. She had me stuck by a mound of dirt that was left from the construction of the McDonald's. I didn't know what to think or expect, so I just sat in my car with my windows up, doors locked, looking in my rearview mirror. For a while, she sat in her car parked behind me, blowing her horn and cursing me out. When she got out, all I heard were her fists hitting the windows of my car. I didn't want her to think I was afraid, even though I was, so I started laughing, which triggered her to continue hitting the car windows and kicking the side doors as if she was trying to get in the car to take my life away.

"If you damage my car, I will call the police!" I yelled, but she didn't care. She continued beating on my car until she hurt her hand, and then she even blamed that on me.

Shortly after, she got back in her car and drove off. I never heard from her again after that day. I felt bad for her, because I realized that if I hadn't gone to prom with her or had sex with her as we were playing being in a relationship, she wouldn't have allowed her emotions to take over.

Soul ties are real, and feelings can sometimes be overbearing, especially if the person you're interested in is not interested in you. From this, I learned that you must discipline yourself and set expectations and boundaries at the beginning of a friendship or potential relationship, so that no one will have to guess where you stand, whether as a friend or as a couple. On the other hand, I had to be honest with myself and realize that I was hurt after losing the friendship that I'd thought would last a lifetime.

At this time in my life, I was constantly asking myself, "Who am I, and am I the man I was created to be?" One day, I was up; the next day, I was down. I often tried to pretend like there wasn't anything boiling inside of me, but there was. Hiding just kept folks from asking questions, but why should I have cared how they felt? Did they care about my feelings? It was my sexuality at the end of the day.

I used to be afraid of what others thought about me, but now I don't care. We all have things to work on in our lives. I am that adopted little boy who went through a lot of resentment growing up. I am that individual who is still dealing with hurt from not meeting or having a positive relationship with all my brothers and sisters. I am that church boy who would miss out on sleep to sit in a church pew bright and early.

I am the Christian who didn't mind praying for the sick and shut-in or visiting the elderly on Saturday mornings.

I know that I am imperfectly perfect, because if I wasn't, Jesus wouldn't have had to get on that cross for sinners like me. Often, I wonder if I am that individual who is doing everything that I am told so I can just "get by." Or am I the one who doesn't mind taking the flight of stairs, step-by-step, through pain and confusion to ensure I make it to the finish line equipped with all the necessities needed for life? I always knew there were no shortcuts to success.

Am I who I want to be? That successful African American with a vision and a platform who can move mountains? Or am I defined by my skin color and my character? We are still facing racism, anti-immigration, homophobia, hate, and other meaningless tactics that disturb the peace. I am a citizen within the United States, living amongst people with a divided mindset. I'm always at the table, for I don't want anyone picking and choosing over me on the menu created by the system, controlled by the government.

I am no longer that person who was once afraid to open because I knew there were people in the world who would tell my secrets. Now, I've been liberated from this fear and don't mind telling the story of how I made it. I am that young boy who tried to fit in, so no one could point me out, but now I am free to do as I please. I wasn't sure at the time, but I know who I am now. I also know that I am fearfully and wonderfully made.

This experience taught me a lot about myself: what I believed as a human being, the values that I hold dear, what love truly is (and isn't), and the ability to make wise decisions that are in my own best interest. From then on, I made a declaration that I would stay out of toxic situations before anyone got hurt mentally, emotionally, and physically.

MIDNIGHT

Growing up in my home, I only had two best friends that never left my side or betrayed me. Nancy and Midnight. Midnight was truly the best friend that I needed to get through the lonely nights. I was only ten years old, but he was truly a man's best friend. Nancy lived next door, at my aunt's house. She was also in foster care.

One night, while watching Extreme Makeover Home Edition, an advertisement came up about a man's best friend. They were referring to a dog. Peanut and I started telling Mama how much we wanted a dog. We knew her first reaction would be no, but Peanut was able to persuade Mama to get the dog. We never knew what kind of dog we wanted, but we knew that we didn't want a Pit Bull or a Rottweiler. Even if we did, we wouldn't have mentioned it to Mama; she was raised to be terrified of those dogs.

She never said if we could get a dog or not, but we knew that if we did get one, it would take time. We were still foster youth. The Department of Children and Families had to do a background check on the dog, and Mama would have to go through a tedious process to ensure she met all policies and procedures to own a dog.

The next week, Mama told Peanut and I that she was expecting a representative from the department to come out and inspect the house to see if we could get a dog. As the caseworker was inspecting the house, she wanted to know what kind of dog Mama was interested in getting, where he would sleep, eat, and many other questions. I was convinced the caseworker had never owned a dog by the questions she was asking.

We knew that Mama didn't have the answers, because she'd never sat down with Peanut and I to talk about getting a dog. Nevertheless, the representative informed Mama that we were "good to go;" we had passed the inspection. Peanut and I were smiling from ear to ear. We knew that we were one step closer to getting a dog.

Mama told us not to ask about it or we wouldn't get one at all, so Peanut and I kept our mouths closed. Weeks went by, and there was still no sign of a dog. We went into our local store to get groceries, and they had dog food on sale. We mentioned it to Mama, and she didn't give us a reply.

As we prepared to put the groceries in the trunk of the car, Mama yelled, "Don't go in my trunk, I repeat, don't go in my trunk!"

We were both confused because usually we put our groceries in there. The only time she would tell us to not go in her trunk was around Christmas time. However, we followed her command and put the groceries in between the seats so we wouldn't make her mad.

The next morning, school was in session. First, Mama had to take us to school and her sister to work since her car wasn't working. On the way to the school, our aunt was complaining about how her car was always giving her issues, something we had known for a while. Her burgundy Quest was very old. You could hear her van coming from miles away. I knew that her car wouldn't last long, because she had to pull over on side streets to put water in her car when it ran hot. Also, the sliding door window always came off, so we either had to hold it with our index finger while she was driving or tie it with a shoelace. Nancy was so embarrassed.

When school let out, we went to the afterschool program. I was sitting on the stairs waiting for Mama to come get us, but she didn't arrive at her usual time. I thought she forgot about Peanut and me, so I began to get worried; her job was right down the street. The Boys & Girls Club closed at six p.m.; it was fifteen minutes before that time but still no sign of Mama. About five minutes after six, Mama came driving like a bat out of hell trying to get us before a late fee would be added to her monthly bill. When she opened her car door, we heard a dog barking. Peanut and I stared at each other, shocked and excited, wondering if what we heard was true.

We'd both raced to the car to see if we were right, and we were! He was very small, with black hair and glossy black eyes. We knew our new dog was just as excited as we were, because he was trying to get out of the cage. When Mama came back in the car, she was smiling, knowing our dream had come true.

On our way to pick up our auntie from her job, she allowed us to let him out of the cage, and he started running all over us. He didn't have a name yet, so we were all debating in the car until we got home to figure out what his name would be. For a while, we would call out random names to see how he would respond. We didn't know what kind of response we were waiting on but all he would do was look around.

When we got home, Peanut carried him in the house, and Mama got on the computer to browse the internet so we could find a meaningful name. A few days later, we all came up with the name "Midnight." He had so much curly black hair, and he would snuggle with one of us in the bed at night, so we knew we had named him right.

No one we knew had much knowledge of how to train him, so we used Google and training pamphlets that we picked up from the local veterinarian office to help guide us. Since he was a Poodle-Chihuahua mix, we found out it would be more difficult to train him, but we tried our best.

Peanut created a schedule for him to eat breakfast, lunch, and dinner, as well as one for him to go outside and play. There weren't any gates surrounding the house, so we couldn't just open the door and let him out, nor did we want him to get hurt or lost in the woods.

Day after day, we fell more in love with him. There wasn't anything we wouldn't do for him, and Peanut took it to the extreme. He would French kiss the dog. When Mama saw Peanut kissing Midnight, she would pretend as if she was about to throw up.

I loved waking up in the middle of the night with Midnight snuggled under my covers with me. It comforted me and made me feel great on the inside. He never failed to wake everyone up in the morning. He would go from room to room and jump on everyone's bed, or he would whine and scratch on the door, wanting to go out and use the bathroom. He would only grow to weigh about thirteen pounds, which Mama thought was perfect.

At dinner time, he went to everyone's chair, begging for human food, even though he had already eaten. Mama kept her eye on us to make sure we didn't sneak him food. She would yell at him to get out the kitchen, and he would look at her then go hide under the kitchen table and sit down. When Mama wasn't looking, Peanut or I would slide food under the table, so he could eat with us.

We loved playing hide and seek, going on walks, playing tricks, or even rubbing Midnight's belly. We did all that we could for him because he was everything to us. He filled a void within our lives; he was like the missing piece in the puzzle. He kept us sane, kept us feeling loved, something we needed to feel, especially after going through so much. He was our best friend; if anyone had an issue with him, they would have to go through us to resolve it.

Years down the road, Mama was asked to keep more foster children, which ordinarily wouldn't have been a problem. But now that we had a dog, they informed her that he must either leave the premises or be put outside; new foster children were terrified of dogs. On the inside, my heart was crushed, and it felt as if my soul had been stabbed by my past once again. They were trying to take away the very thing that gave me peace and made me feel special. He showed me love by the way he'd cuddle up with me in the bed at night after having a long evening of playing with him and taking him on long-tiring walks. He protected me if he felt I was in danger.

We knew that he wasn't leaving the premises, and we weren't going to put him outside in the yard either. Hell! He was only thirteen pounds; no one should fear a dog that small, I thought to compromise, Mama cleaned off her new closed-in back porch, and we made him a home out there. I was content but still upset. It didn't feel the same. I felt a disconnect, and I knew that Midnight felt abandoned, but there wasn't anything we could do. Peanut or I went out there with him daily, and we agreed that we would take turns sweeping and mopping the porch once a week.

The first night he stayed on the porch, no one could sleep. He was scratching on the door for hours. I knew he was in emotional pain. I went out there and rubbed his stomach, because he'd be breathing hard, eyes blinking as if he wanted to cry. He didn't have much freedom anymore. Peanut started getting angry at Mama because he knew what our dog was going through, and it seemed as if no one cared.

When no one was home except for Peanut and I, we would open the back door and let him in the house. We didn't care if Mama got upset; we were not going to abandon the very thing that meant the world to us. We would close all the bedroom and bathroom doors, so he could roam only in the main rooms When we would have to put him back on the back porch, he'd make that face your dog makes when you are getting ready to leave the house, heartbreaking, right?

A few years later, we knew that something wasn't right when our dog would often stop eating his food and drinking his water. We couldn't figure out what was going on, so we took him to the veterinarian to get checked out. He had an ear infection and was prescribed two types of medication. One for his ears, the other for his appetite since he had lost a few pounds.

He got better but then got sick again. Each time the report and prescriptions were different. Mama believed it was old age—he was nine years old. I was convinced it was because he was forced to live on the back porch, which wasn't in the best condition anymore. The screen had holes in it, which allowed for bugs to get in. I got heated because I knew that the foundation for all this nonsense was the Department of Children and Families. Had he still been able to live in the house, we wouldn't have had to deal with this nonsense. Mama felt the heaviness on my heart by the way I spoke to her and the caseworker when she inspected the house.

This overbearing caseworker comes to our home and nitpicks over things that don't pertain to the central reason why she came. If she isn't worried that someone is staying in the home that will not get a background check, or worried that the dog roams around the house when she leaves the premises. She persists in coming to the home and possibly surprising Mama just to do a "Check-in". Mama would get pissed. No, she didn't have everything in order all the time, but what she did make sure was that the foster kids that were under her care were in good hands and had the necessities that they needed.

As time went on, Mama couldn't continue to afford to pay for Midnight's veterinarian visits, so she sat Peanut and I down and asked us what she should do with him. We didn't have much to say, because we knew which direction she was headed. We also knew that she had already made the decision for him to go to the shelter.

The next morning felt like darkness had come over the earth. It was gloomy and wet outside; the sun wasn't shining, and the clouds were dark in color. It was a sad day. Mama was packing up Midnight's belongings and putting his things in the trunk of her car. Peanut and I didn't help; we were hurt. On the trip to the shelter, we held him tight, kissing all over him and praying for him. He would only look at us and then look down. I felt as if my mind was slipping. I couldn't understand why Peanut and I had to go through this.

When Mama parked the car outside of the shelter, we helped unpacked his things and took him inside the building. Mama told Peanut and I that someone would eventually adopt him, but she didn't know that I overheard her speaking to a friend of the family stating that he would be put down after a few months.

Although I was angry, I decided to be grateful for the memories that I was able to have with him. Midnight was an integral and irreplaceable part of my family, with a personality that is unique, loveable and utterly unforgettable. I wish I could have said goodbye for the last time before he was put down, or, take him on to our favorite nature trail at Tom Brown Park--but anger was building up and I didn't know how to release the emotions that I was feeling within.

When I asked the staff at the shelter if I could see where he would be housed, they laughed and told me he would be locked in a cage. I knew from that day forward that he would not have any freedom. Peanut and I said our final goodbyes. Before we walked out the door, the staff promised they would take good care of him, but we both knew they would say anything to comfort us. A few minutes later, we drove off. I looked out the back window, praying that Midnight would run outside.

He never did.

I never saw him again after that day, but I always thought of him. I promised myself that I would never go back to the dog shelter that put my best friend to sleep, but any time I passed by it going to school, going in town, or going to work, Midnight was the first thing that would come to mind. A piece of me was still with him. My stomach would squeeze tight, and I would wonder what really happened to him. Did he really get put down, or, did he get adopted by another family? Years had gone by without seeing him or hearing him panting after a long run or barking just to alert me that something just may not be right. I even went to some dog parks to see if a new owner had gotten him. When I called his name, the other dog owners in the park would look at me as if I didn't belong there. I didn't come with a dog.

Once, I saw a woman whose dog looked just like Midnight, so I ran to her to see if that could be him.

"No, I'm sorry, sir, you have the wrong dog."

I left the park and rode around town until I decided to go back to the dog shelter.

When I entered the doors of the building, the staff asked, "How can I help you today?"

I went on to ask if they kept records of the dogs, they took in. I was instructed to go next door for help with that. Next door, they asked for my driver's license along with many questions to ensure that I was who I said I was. I didn't know if they'd take me seriously. I was twenty years-old, practically grown, asking about a dog? I thought. Finally, they found his records.

"What is it that you would like to know?"

"I would like to know what happened to him when we left."

The staff member looked at me and sighed. She would have to go through hundreds of files to find this information.

I stood there with my eyes wide open, waiting for her to talk. I noticed that spit was forming on the creases of her lips. She tried to lick her lips but ended up drooling on the paper. I went on to ask, "Is everything okay?" She nodded her head before speaking.

"He was brought in on October 14, 2010. We assessed him the next morning, and he would not cooperate with any of the staff. All he was doing was growling, biting, and barking at us. Being that he wasn't cooperating, we gave him some liquid that would put him to sleep. We checked on him before sunrise...that's when he died." I was shaking. The woman saw my reaction and apologized.

Lastly, she went on to tell me that they cremated him and threw his ashes in the dumpster—as this is something that is so natural that a dog owner should just understand. This made me feel like he didn't mean anything to her, or anyone that took part in the process. They didn't know Midnight the way I knew him, and Midnight wasn't with them growing up in the wee hours of the mornings licking all over their face as he would do with Peanut and I because it was a dawn of a new day.

I couldn't do anything but leave the building. I was broken and there was nothing I could do even if I tried. All I could think about was his soulful eyes that would have pleaded with me to help him, one breath at a time until his last. Or, his thin tail tucked between his legs as he would stand still with fear on the table that was prepared for his death.

To this day, I have not lost one memory of Midnight. It still seems surreal and although I am grateful for Mama to take in children—including Peanut and me, I wish she would have stopped once she adopted the both of us. I am sure Midnight would have been with us for more years and not closed in on a screen-porch.

I know the pain many others feel when their pet, whether it's a dog or not, dies. It's a feeling that separates the world you once lived in, to the reality of what is. I may just get a new dog anytime, but a new dog will not replace the feelings or make me feel better—it will only make me feel worse.

THE CHURCH HOUSE

On Sundays, there wasn't a single question of what the plans for the day was, because we always knew— school and morning worship. If we had any plans for Sundays, they were cancelled. Even if we didn't want to follow Mama's plans, we had no choice but to do so, because she would always remind us: "You have one job in this house; that is to go to school, graduate, and get a job. Y'all don't pay one bill, and you have food on your table each day, so if you thought that you weren't going to listen, then you got the wrong one." If we hadn't been delivered from all our sins and wrongdoings by the time Sunday night came around, we would need to "lay on the altar," as Mama would say. Even if we didn't know we had sinned, Mama was convinced that God wasn't pleased.

We would wake up early to gospel music or listening to an older preacher on the cassette player delivering a sermon. If the cassette would stop working, she'd have Peanut or I turn on her black Sony portable radio that would only turn on if she put duct-tape around the batteries, because if not, they would always pop out. During this time, breakfast was being prepared, if not already completed. We were expected to freshen up, put on our church socks, slacks, shoes and undershirt so we could be three-fourths dressed before we sat down to eat. I knew better than to put on the collared shirt she'd ironed the night before eating. If I spilled food on it, she'd be livid.

Sunday breakfasts were always great. We would have grits, eggs, sausage, bacon, and pancakes. We would be in service for most of the day, so Mama made her grits buttery and thick, so it would "stick to our stomachs." When finished, we'd clean up our spot, brush our teeth again, and put on our collared shirts, so we could attend Sunday school and morning worship. Though Mama tried to get us to Sunday school on time, we were always late. Sometimes, she would throw on a nightgown and drop Peanut and me off then rush back home to get ready for service.

The first three Sundays in every month were regular morning worship services. But the fourth Sunday, my favorite Sunday in each month, was the youth department program. The church always believed in investing in and empowering youth, so our youth director created a program where only young adults would speak. We'd open in praise and worship; the entire church still supported us, even though we sounded hideous. Some worshiped through praise dance or helped with the offering collection. I was always on program, either presiding over the service or giving the opening prayer. Some Sundays, I would mime dance, a gift that I never knew I had in me until the dance coordinator told me that I needed to showcase my skills.

Sunday school was in an old, cold room, steps away from the baptism pool or dipping pool —what I like to call it. I remember trying to stay focused on the teacher during the lesson, but it was challenging. There were too many things going on, from other people's children playing around kicking each other's shoes under the table, to children walking in and out of the classroom, to people playing on their phones. It wasn't an actual learning environment, and the teachers who taught the class knew it as well.

When it was time for dismissal, a silver collection tray was passed around, which I never understood, because as children we didn't have any money, and if we did have money (from allowance), it wasn't going towards offering. But now that I have gotten older and wiser, I wish I would have given the small change that I had. I would be further along in my success had I sown/ I do know that when God allows you to have your harvest season, it is bountiful.

The most offering I gave as a child was one dollar. Sometimes, Mama would have extra money and would give fifty cents for Sunday school and one dollar for church. The Sunday school teacher didn't have time to count the money given, so a student volunteer was needed. I liked money, so I didn't mind counting it, even though it wasn't coming back to me.

Once the money had been collected and accounted for, I would count the number of youths in attendance. On youth Sundays, we'd have more children than usual. On typical Sundays, the same youth could be counted on to be in attendance: my household and my aunt from next door. We were known for always attending Sunday school and for always having foster children; it wouldn't be right if we weren't there.

After counting the attendees, as a class we would discuss what we'd learned from the lesson, and what we were going to present to all the attendees at Sunday school. No one ever wanted to go first to present what they had learned, not even myself. We weren't Bible scholars, and, more than likely, we had been playing around during the review. And we'd forget what we were going to say during the presentation anyway. After the presentation, we received applause and feedback, then Sunday school would be over. Immediately after, we would transition into the morning worship service. By that time, other members and guests were coming inside to be seated.

Church always started with an old-school hymn. One of my favorites was "A Charge to Keep I Have." Afterwards, we would go into praise and worship, then the sermon, and dismissal. Seems very fast, right? Well, that's not the reality. Most Sundays, the service included many praise breaks throughout, which made the service longer. Then, the Pastor would give a long, drawn-out word that would make you feel like he knew your life like the back of his hand. After the word, there would be an altar call, and then dismissal.

We never left immediately. Mama always had meetings to attend. At one point, we were at church for two hours before service started and stayed two hours after to clean up the toddler room Mama had started. She named the program "King's Kids," a place where babies, toddlers, and children up to age six could come during service. This way, parents could concentrate on the service while their child received a similar, age-appropriate lesson. She had reliable adults and teenagers who rotated as teachers on Sundays.

After Mama felt her assignment was complete, we would go home. The radio would still be playing. At times, I wanted to throw the whole thing away, with its annoying search for a signal. Eventually, Mama would get tired of her gospel tunes not playing clearly, so she'd turn them off and lie down to rest. Once she got up, we'd eat dinner. She only cooked dinner on Saturdays. She didn't believe in cooking a full-course dinner on Sunday, because she believed in rest on the Sabbath. We'd eat leftovers. She loved giving options, so she would cook two types of meat and several sides. The food she cooked would have to last the entire week—and she would make sure it did.

Once Sunday was over, we would get back to our regular routine. If we weren't at school or a community function, we were at church for something. Throughout the week, we either had youth choir practice, mime dance practice, tutoring, or visiting with the elderly.

As a little boy, my church family always called me "preacher." When I got older, I hated when people called me that, because I wasn't a preacher, and didn't anticipate becoming one—unless God says otherwise. One of our church friends, who was known for baking delicious cakes, invited Mama and I to her house to get some cake and to watch some video clips from church when we were younger. She played so many videos, including and old one of me. I was three years old and in the annual Christmas play. I was a short, chubby bow-legged toddler acting as if I was the pastor, jumping up and down on the chair, squealing, trying to give a Christmas word about the real reason we celebrate Christmas. Everyone in the room was laughing as tears rolled down their eyes. From that play on, everyone else felt I was called to spread God's word.

After having an in-depth conversation with my biological mother once after was freed from the abuse of liquor and drugs, she shared with me how the "church folks" treated her when she was sober after being drunk. They'd roll their eyes at her, refusing to give her a ride to or from church, and some would even speak negative things to her when she did find a ride to church. I could feel the pain by the way she was telling me how she was being treated. She admitted that she has a drug issue. She didn't expect to be so criticized by the people who were faithful churchgoers, and ones who led everyone to believe their lives were perfect. I am not blaming or criticizing the church, but there should be nothing wrong with receiving guidance from people who are doing well if they can help someone in need—my mother at the time. It's not of God to pray for someone to be delivered from their issues, then start talking about them.

Despite the issues my biological mother faced, she knew that going to church and receiving a "on-time word," as she would say, was needed. One on the things she liked most about my adoptive mother is that she always kept us in church. From the good singing, stomping, and shouting, everyone had the opportunity to ignite positive change and a fresh wind in their life—especially if they were there for the right reasons.

I remember the time I was seated in a pew next to Mama, and she caught the Holy Ghost. I was terrified and had to move until she calmed down. One of her arms was wrapped around her stomach, the other behind her back as she jumped up and down. Usually, an usher would have to come fan her to calm her down. The lesson for that Sunday was themed around Joshua and the gates of Jericho. This was a biblical story about how the gates were locked down due to the Israelites. During this time, no one went out or came in. God then spoke to Joshua and gave him the responsibility marching around the city once every day until the seventh day. And, on that day, Joshua would have to walk around the city seven times as the priests were blowing their trumpets, and the wall of the city would soon fall, so they could enter.

Pastor reminded us that just as those walls were standing up tall, firm and strong, we, too, have walls that are just as tall and strong that need to come down. I didn't understand where he was going with the message, because there was no way he knew everything about my life, past and present But, this word was "on-time." As I compared his message to my own life, I realized I had so many walls, some built myself or some built by others. They were blocking me from receiving my next breakthrough or blessing. The walls I had up were what I thought protection from getting hurt from rejection, because I was afraid of being who I really was, and I didn't want to be judged by others. I also didn't want to face the truth about the situations I was put in. I knew that it was ultimately up to me to bring those walls down, however, I knew that I would have to allow God to order my steps, as it is not an easy process.

That same day I gave my life to God. I made the decision to be baptized—the best decision I made in my life. I had to confess my sins so that I could be born again in Christ. I knew that if I wanted to be a real follower of Christ, I needed to make the right steps, and the first step was to get aligned with the man that created me, God.

Later that month, the pastor, ministers, evangelists, mothers, and deacons of the church, along with my family and friends gathered around the baptism pool so they could witness the event. While I was at the altar, there were many people surrounding me. I could hear people crying and praising the Lord that I made the right decision. My only concern was the cold water I would have to be placed in to complete the baptism process.

I started feeling lightheaded as one foot stepped in front of the other into the pool. The farther I went, the more lightheaded and nervous I became. The water was so cold, my shoulders started shaking. Mama was right there, sitting at the edge of the pool in tears, praising God. Peanut was in the corner by Mama, holding his face as if something scary was going to happen.

For about fifteen minutes, many people started giving testimonies while I was in the water—they were happy that a child like me decided to give his life to Christ. Mama's testimony was about how she prayed for this day to come, and how God answered them. Other testimonies were about how children and young adults get lost in the world through violence, drugs, locked-up in jail; but on that day I decided to be found. If I could tell them to hush, I would have. The water was very cold, and I just wanted to get out. I knew it wasn't Christ-like, so I stood there shivering with most of my body submerged in water and listened to others.

Finally, the Pastor stopped everyone from talking so he could baptize me. I knew he was cold, too, because he whispered, "We need a warm baptism pool." When the pastor prepared to dip me in the water, all I heard was, "I baptize you in the name of the Father, the name of the Son, and the name of the Holy Ghost," before I opened my eyes to everyone shouting and crying. We all rejoiced because I was now deemed a part of the Lord's body. My pastor started singing one of my favorite songs "Heavy Load", because I had finally gotten rid of my "Heavy Load." Everyone in the room experienced a rekindling of love to God for all he has done for not only myself, but for everyone in making me part of the new covenant through repentance and faith.

UNCOMMON THINGS

Through church and work, I made several friends. At least, I thought I did. In my circle of friends, there were leeches and leaders. Leeches would leave after they tried to suck everything out of me, but leaders would keep me moving in the right direction. I rarely had friends come over to the house--not because I couldn't have them over, but because I was embarrassed. I overheard different conversations about how big my classmates' houses were and how they could go swimming anytime they liked, but all I had was a swing set and a basketball goal with the net hanging halfway off. There was no cement that I could play ball on, only sand and small patches of grass. One thing I was grateful for was that Mama's house was on a lot of land surrounded by trees, so we didn't have any noisy neighbors, nor did we have to hear the loud sirens of police cars, ambulances or fire trucks; the trees kept us closed off and free.

Staying outside for a long period of time never occurred to me. I always found some excuse to go inside. Though I didn't have the special amenities that my friends had, I knew Mama tried her best. Most times, Peanut and I weren't even home. When all our schedules were clear, we were at the mall shopping or cruising around the city.

If we didn't have anything else, we had a mama and a home filled with pure love and joy. There was not a single time love wasn't displayed. Even when I got whooping's growing up, she'd always say,

"Now, if I didn't love you, I'd let you do whatever. But I do love you, and that means that I will have to correct and discipline you when you are wrong." I believed Mama every time she said that, except when she used her wooden meter stick or grabbed anything in her reach to throw at me. The bad part was that whatever she tried to hit me with always broke, and she'd get even more upset because I didn't get hit with the item. I'd laugh in her face, because I couldn't understand why she would waste her energy trying to discipline me; whooping me didn't make me get any better.

Peanut always told me stories of how our biological mother never spanked us because she was too busy doing other things. Perhaps that was the reason we both threw temper tantrums throughout the separation, and why we were labeled as "out of control" by some people. Those same people who labeled us didn't know anything about us, so what they believed, and thought didn't matter. During this time, my biological mother was in and out of jail, when she was out of jail, she was off crack cocaine. However, she would often get drunk.

Growing up, I was a mama's boy. I was spoiled from the time I stepped into the house I would eventually call home. Mama had three children of her own: Victoria, Aaron and Aymin. Her oldest daughter passed away right before I arrived at the house. Aaron had a mental issue, as I am not certain of the diagnosis he had; I am pretty sure it was on the lines of Intermittent Explosive Disorder (ISD).The Department of Children and Families would not allow him to be around any children that Mama kept due to his record. Mama didn't want to leave him hanging, so she would always find ways for him to stay adjacent to our home. When we would see him walking down the roads, as we were in the car going into town, it was hard to tell what was wrong with him. He would walk with his head down, and his face covered enough just so you could see his eyes if you got close to him., no matter who was outside.

I'll never forget the time Mama got new double-pane windows installed. When we left for the day and came back home, Aaron had broken all the windows with cement blocks and wooden poles he'd found in the yard. Mama cried and cried, because she nor the police could understand why he had these episodes. Putting restraining orders and adjunctions on him served no purpose. By the time Aaron found out about the restraining orders or adjunctions, he'd already damaged something else.

Mama didn't believe he knew what he was doing during each episode. He wasn't on his medicine, and he thought everyone was out to get him, though that wasn't the case. Peanut and I lost out on many opportunities because Mama often had to spend money and get the house fixed after one of Aaron's episodes. When she thought she had extra money to take us shopping or do an out-door activity, she would have to use that money to fix something that Aaron had damaged.

Since we had become brothers through the adoption, we needed to love and support him. He was no different from any of us, except when he didn't take his medication. When he was on his medicine, he was friendly, sharing stories about his childhood, he'd help with the chores around the house, and help keep up with the yard. Mama always demonstrated her love to him, even when Peanut, Aymin, and I told her that he took advantage of some of the nice things she did for him. But her love was so deep for him, she couldn't resist. She tried to help him get therapy to gain his independence, and she even got him a small compact RV that was placed behind our house; but that only made matters worse.

After getting his electricity, water, and cable connected he started acting normal for a few months until he needed helping to pay his bills. Mama got tired of paying all the bills by herself when she knew he could chip in a few dollars with his disability check. When she finally decided to speak up about it, he lashed out. Her youngest biological son, Aymin, continued trying to convince her that she needed to stop helping Aaron, but she wouldn't listen to him, either. She didn't believe in showing favoritism to anyone, so she went with whatever her heart told her.

Aymin was doing his own thing in the world. He was in and out of Mamas house at his leisure. He was Mama's biological last child, and the only one who could make something out of himself. Her daughter had passed away, and her oldest struggled with mental health. He tried to make the best of his situation and go to a community college, but he took his acceptance offer for granted. He skipped class, didn't do homework, and put the streets before his education.

I learned then that many students who attend college can receive a refund if their student account reflects a surplus after all tuition and fees are paid. When he received his refund, he thought that it was free money from the government and that he wouldn't have to pay it back. That wasn't the case. He didn't have any scholarships or grants. When Nancy tried to correct him with his misinterpretation of the financial aid letter he'd received, he was in denial. About two months into the semester, he decided that college wasn't for him and dropped out. Along with dropping out, his court record stopped him from being qualified to apply to certain jobs. He liked making quick money without having to put in a lot of work. At the time I didn't know if that was a good or bad thing, but I knew I didn't want to center my life around money. Mama always stated that money is the root of evil. Because of his lack of responsibility with his goals and trying to maintain a job, he moved in and out of the house. Mama would get upset each time she let him back in, because she knew he could do better, but there wasn't anything that she could do anymore but pray for him.

The only two people Mama had to take care of were Peanut and me, unless she had more foster children, which she would get occasionally. Anything we wanted she did her best to get for us. She worked three jobs. She was a foster mother, she worked for the state of Florida and cleaned up office buildings at night. She also received monthly stipends from the state for Peanut and me since she adopted us. She would receive additional monthly stipends if she had foster children. These stipends go toward the care of the children they are fostering or had already adopted. Qualified expenses can include clothing, toys, food, daycare, medical expenses, or anything that she believed was necessary and in the well-being of the child. Sometimes she would be tired and ask for us to help her "knock out the bathrooms and lobbies" in whatever buildings she had to clean up. We would always help, because we wanted her home with us, not cleaning up after people all night. If she was running low on money, she'd "borrow" a few rolls of tissue and paper towels for the house from her jobs, so we wouldn't be without. Though she was busy and came home drained, she still managed to cook a hot meal every night. After eating dinner, I would give Mama a back massage, because she would complain about how her back was sore. There was no time for her to go out and pamper herself, so Peanut and I did what we could.

We were taught that love was the greatest gift of all. I knew what love really meant when I started helping Mama bake cakes at the age of ten, especially around holiday seasons. Baking sounded easy, especially if I could have the recipe in front of me. But it wasn't. It was more than reading a step-by-step recipe or ensuring that all my ingredients were measured just right. I learned that it wasn't a skill that everyone could simply pick up or be trained to do. To get the best results, the talent had to be within me.

When I first started baking, I was only allowed to make cornbread. This would occur on Sunday's right before all the food was warmed up—Mama would cook main dishes the night before. Mama would stand over my shoulder and give me directions. I followed each step. And when I mastered baking cornbread, she began teaching me how to bake cakes.

After I put all the ingredients in the mixing bowl, Mama would give me a lecture about greasing the cake pan so the cake wouldn't stick. I would grease the pan with the wrappers from the stick butter and use cooking oil to be on the safe side, then sprinkle the bottom of the Bundt pan with flour. My biggest fear while learning wasn't ensuring that the cake batter was right but ensuring that the cake would rise while in the oven. If the cake didn't rise, I knew that I had messed up the batter. If it did rise, I knew that I had done everything right.

Once we put the cake in the oven, everyone had to get out of the kitchen until an hour had passed. Mama believed that the cake was going to fall since Peanut and I walked so hard, a rule she had learned as a little girl while her mother was baking cakes. We couldn't allow a cake to fall because of our silly mistakes. The ingredients were expensive, so we did our best to tiptoe through the kitchen when we were baking.

We'd all watch a movie in the den until we smelled the cake, then we would talk about how good it smelled in the house. "It smells like that bakery in Thomasville, Georgia," Mama would say. We would laugh and wait until the timer went off. After taking the cake out of the oven and letting it cool, Mama would shake the cake pan a few times then flip it upside down, so it would come out. She'd then teach me how to make homemade icing for the cake.

After I mastered cakes, Mama let me bake for all major events and holidays. When I first started baking by myself, I put all the ingredients in the mixer at once, so I could hurry up and be done. But the cakes never turned out right. But Mama believed in me and continued to push me. I followed all the instructions given to ensure the cake presentation was a success. From preheating the oven, to sifting the cake flour, to even ensuring that the measurements were exact. I didn't want to let Mama down, so I followed the recipe until I really knew it for myself.

No one could tell me anything about how to bake a cake after a while. I knew those recipes in and out. Mama was known in the community for baking cakes, so I had to make sure my cakes were on point.

After I started receiving praise from people I didn't even know, I invested in myself by purchasing supplies for my growing cake business. Mama purchased a KitchenAid stand mixer, so I wouldn't have to take a long time with the hand-held mixer. It was worth the investment. We started selling cakes by the slice after church on youth Sundays, to raise money for the youth congregation and brand my baking skills. My cake clientele increased significantly because my turn-around time was quick, and the cake was always good. We were sold out in seconds.

After Mama saw my continued success, together we learned how to bake other flavors of cakes. She even went on to teach me how to make sweet potato pies. Before I knew it, we had a pool of customers requesting pies as well.

A few years later, Mama entered me in the community baking competition that our church hosted for the annual church anniversary celebration. I was shy when I found out that I was in the competition, because I knew that some of the bakers in my church had more experience than I did. But Mama wouldn't allow that to stop me from competing. Each weekend up until the competition, I was either at the store purchasing ingredients to make different flavors of cakes and pies or in the kitchen trying new recipes and cake icing designs. Since I was known for my pound cakes, I wanted the judges of the competition and the other competitors to see how diverse I was. After messing up a few new cake recipes I found on Google, I reverted to what I knew by heart, because that would be the only thing I felt comfortable with, especially being that I couldn't cut a slice of the cake to taste it before entering it into the competition.

Mama took off her night job just to watch me make the cake. She encouraged me while I was in the kitchen. Though I thought that the judges would think I was too young to enter, I knew that my skills were advanced, so I prayed my cake wouldn't be overlooked.

The morning of the competition, nervousness kicked in. I didn't know what to think or how to feel because the big day had arrived. All I wanted to do was get the day over with, so I could move beyond the competition. After getting dressed, we left to turn in the cake before the start of the event, so we wouldn't be disqualified. The event was not to start until later in the day. Mama wasn't going to waste her gas by going back to the house until the event started, so we volunteered to help set up tents, tables, and chairs. Most of the items needed were at our church next door. We walked back and forth from the church to the fellowship center, which is where the event was located. The property was originally purchased to be the home of our new church facility; however enough money wasn't raised to pay off the property and construct the new church, so until that happened, we used the property for events, conferences, and meetings.

After turning in my sweets and helping to set up, I noticed that there was one room with a written sign on the door stating, "CAKE COMPETITION JUDGES ONLY." I started sweating in seconds, feeling as if I had already lost. I knocked on the door to ask if I could see the other cakes, but no one answered my knocks. Slowly, I went into the room, and before my eyes there were dozens of cakes lined up. All different shapes, sizes, and flavors. I knew it would be a challenge for the judges, because according to the rules of the competition, the judges had to sample each cake to score it correctly. I didn't know who submitted what cake into the competition, because all the names were taken off each cake to be fair. As time went on, cars started turning into the entrance of the house.

At two o'clock, the event coordinators announced that the judges were starting to sample each cake, so we should get prepared to hear the verdict of the competition. Immediately, I went to the bathroom and waited there until I felt like the verdict was in. I didn't want to hear that I hadn't won. I would feel embarrassed and defeated, especially being the youngest competitor.

Minutes later, I heard voices yelling my name. I didn't know what that meant, so I came out of my hiding place. When people saw me, they were overjoyed, because I had won the cake bake-off competition. Also, I learned that I had placed second in the sweet potato pie category. I didn't enter the sweet potato pie competition, so I was confused about how I'd placed at all. I ran up to Mama to give her a hug and thank her for keeping me focused on getting the job done, and she told me that she'd taken a sweet potato pie from the freezer that I'd made a few weeks prior and entered it on my behalf.

After the event, many people asked if I could bake them a cake. Of course, I told them that I could, but the prices had to go up. I started charging thirty dollars per cake and fifteen dollars for a sweet potato pie. I thought I was asking too much, however after doing calculations, I realized that I was giving a great deal, because I wasn't profiting much after buying ingredients.

Around Easter, Thanksgiving, and Christmas, I increased the prices of the cakes and pies, because demand was greater. During those peak times, Mama would help me, so I could get the cakes delivered on time. I believed in quality customer service.

I knew that God placed me in the right household one day when I was cleaning the kitchen after baking cakes. Mama came over and showed me the Mother's Day booklet I had made for her when I was in the second grade. She stood in the corner of the kitchen, smiling and talking to herself about how far I'd come along and matured, despite what other people thought of me. She told me that sometimes people would tell her that I would end up in juvenile detention, or that she would have wanted to send me back to foster care.

The book was laminated with a bright pink cover. On the front of the book was a picture of Mama and me that we'd taken during orientation before school had started my second-grade year. She was wearing her clothes for the night cleaning job. I was wearing a green shirt and blue jeans.

Looking at the picture, I could tell that she was overwhelmed with working multiple jobs and still supporting her children at different events. The next page was a table of contents that I put together in the order that I thought was best fit for the type of booklet that it was. Going through the pages was a certificate of appreciation for being the greatest mother ever, with a pledge of things that I'd promised to do: brush my hair, clean my room, sweep the floor—all the things that she'd taught me how to do in my early days. The next page was my creativity piece. I was able to draw my mom's favorite place in the house, which I believed was the kitchen. I thought it was ironic that she was sharing with me the booklet I'd made years before in the very room I'd called her favorite place in the house. Out of all the pages that I'd taken my time to make, my favorite section was "What My Mother Means to Me." And it went like this:

My mom helps me with my homework
When I need help on a problem.
My mom does things for me like
take me out and eat wherever I
want to go. She lets me go to me
favorite places like Georgia and on
a cruise. My mom cooks food and
buys my favorite thing and cleans
up. My mom is the sweetest mom.
Love, Jacari Harris

I wondered how she could even read anything in the booklet. My second-grade handwriting was horrible. But the best part is that my handwriting didn't matter to her. She told me that she didn't care about the skill of writing, because any skill could be taught. She cared about the impact that I'd made, and she was impacted by the work that I'd completed for her.

POP

A man who can turn a woman's life around for the better is what I call a real man. This male figure wasn't always in my life, but he came right on time.

My biological mother had eight children before she met this man and was soon pregnant with her ninth child by him. They had known each other since the late eighties but had never been in a relationship. I was nine years old when they first started dating. He lived next door to my grandma (which is where my biological mother stayed). He was a native and lifelong resident of Tallahassee and a disabled U.S. Army veteran who'd served during the Vietnam War. He had two homes and three cars.

In July of 2004, my mother was sentenced to prison for aggravated assault with a deadly weapon. After she was released from prison, she decided to get in a committed relationship with her long-time friend, Pop. Shortly after, she got pregnant she no longer wanted to reside in Florida. So, she ventured off to Boston to live with some family with the hopes of being able to get out on her own and make a living for her and newly expected infant. Though she was pregnant by her new boyfriend, she didn't care at the time that he stayed behind in Florida. However, when he told her to come back to Florida, so he could marry her and take care of their daughter, she packed her bags and moved back to Florida to live with him. I was ten years.

When my biological mother arrived back to Florida, she started back visiting with Peanut and I when she could. If she couldn't, we knew that she was back in jail. Mama thought since she rekindled an old relationship with Pop and had a baby with him that she was off to a better start, but she was still in and out of jail frequently.

Mama was afraid to let us stay with her, but she was also glad that our biological mother was gradually changing for the better—when she wasn't behind bars. The weekends that our biological mother was free, Peanut and I would get up early to be dropped off to spend the day with her and Pop. We knew that Mama didn't have to allow visitation with our biological mother because she had adopted us and had jurisdiction of what we could do.

The house by Grandma's was so small, you could knock into something anytime you moved around. It was just big enough for our new sister, our mother, and her new husband, Pop. Peanut and I would watch TV with Pop whenever we stayed there. A few of our other siblings would come over as well if their adoptive families let them. He liked to watch shows like The Price is Right and Judge Mathis. Mama would yell at the plaintiff and defendant throughout the Judge Mathis show, because she believed they were lying. Or, Peanut and I would listen to her rant on the laws that both the defendant and plaintiff broke and how she had been in similar situations in her life.

For lunch, we ate cold cuts, chips and drank Kool-Aid or Coke in a mason jar filled with ice. Pop loved a bologna sandwich. Our biological mother, Freddie-Mae, would get a round frying pan with a spoonful of butter to fry the bologna. Peanut and I would laugh at them, because we had never seen anyone fry bologna. After the bologna was done, she'd get two slices of potato bread, pile mayonnaise on both sides, then add lettuce, cheese, and two slices of tomato. Before she closed the sandwich, she'd pour salt and pepper over the top. Peanut would shake his head in disbelief, and I would always question their health, because I knew too much salt intake could lead to high blood pressure.

After they woke up from their noon nap, we'd go on a ride in Pop's red Ford Explorer, or, if everyone was in a good mood, we'd walk around the block to the corner store. Every time we went there, we would get kicked out by the owner. He wasn't racist; he just didn't want my mother stealing from them anymore, which she always did before meeting Pop.

Some days she decided to be the bigger person and not go into the store. Instead, she'd tell Pop to loan her a few dollars to give to Peanut and me, so we could get whatever we wanted. I don't know why she called it a loan since she never paid him back, but he always gave it to her. On our walk back to their house, she'd point out different houses and apartment complexes that we use to stay in, or we would stop by a friend of hers who watched us when we were babies while she was working.

Months later, they decided to give up the house right next to our grandma's and move to their second house across town; they had more space there plus a front and back yard. Mama felt better taking us there, because the home had more space, the yard was bigger, and it was a closer commute for us. She wasn't concerned about working, Pop was a retired Veteran—and if you don't know anything about a Veteran, their benefits are second to none, and they receive a hefty check each month. He told me that his only job was to take care of my mother and little sister, and if they were happy, he was happy—and they were happy! Pop started taking her to church though she stopped doing illegal drugs, her drinking never ceased. Yet, we continued getting calls at all hours of the night where she would cry, yell at us, and tell us, "You and Peanut are coming back home with me! I already prayed to my Jesus about it, and he has shown me how it will happen."

Mama would tell us to hang up the phone, because we didn't need to hear anything she had to say. I'd hang up, because I didn't want to upset Mama. The next morning, we would get an apology call from our mother, but we never took it seriously, because we were accustomed to her doing it. Our mother wanted all nine of her children to get together at her house and have a crab boil and grill food, something that, according to my older brothers and sisters, she loved to do before the separation. She had all my siblings contact numbers, so she called everyone and asked if they'd be interested. She knew that if we wanted to come, it would influence our adoptive parents to let us time with her and our other siblings. After she called Peanut and me, we were excited, and Mama had already said yes since we had mentioned that we were expecting a call to get invited. I called my other siblings just to be sure that they could come as well—which they all said that they could.

Two weeks later, on a hot Saturday Morning—the day we could visit with our biological mother and siblings, Peanut and I got up very early so we could be the first ones to arrive. All my other siblings started getting dropped off minutes after each other, just in time for us to go to the store and get all the things we needed for the crab boil. We walked to Family Dollar together in the hot scorching sun, while Pop went to go get the crabs from the seafood market. Our mother's driving privileges were revoked from a years-ago DUI, so she was accustomed to walking or catching the bus to go get things that she needed. While walking to Family Dollar we all were updating each other on how we were doing in school and listening to Mama tell us how she'd be able to get us back for good. We'd listen, and encourage her that she would be able to, but deep down we knew that there was no way for her to get us back because her parental rights were taken away.

Once we left Family Dollar to go back to the house, we stopped by the candy lady house to get flips—or frozen Kool-Aid to cool us off on our walk back from the store. Soon, Pop arrived with the blue crabs. Everyone wanted to help cook them except for me. I was afraid that I would get clamped; I knew how it felt from previous experience. I liked hearing them move around in the bag... until the crabs tore through it and started crawling out. I started yelling at the top of my lungs then ran outside to help my mother grill the shrimp and chicken. She wrapped the shrimp in aluminum foil with a beer coating, then I helped by putting the barbeque sauce on both the shrimp and chicken.

We ate all day long until it was time to go home. Though we didn't want to leave each other, we knew we had to. We didn't get many moments together, but when we did, we lived our best lives. Pop did all he could for our mother, and the daughter that they had together, Jamie. At the time she was seven years old. He took good care of Peanut, my other siblings, and I as well; until the day he died.

I remember that Friday morning, I was in 10th grade sitting in my Drawing II elective course, complaining to the teacher how cold I was. We were doing a project that required the room's temperature to be cool and the lights to be off so their brightness wouldn't affect the work that we were doing. I started playing on my phone under the desk while the teacher wasn't looking. I knew I was wrong, because she had posters on each wall of the classroom that had a large red X over a cell phone. She would say, "Please put your phone away before class starts" to ensure that she had our undivided attention. This day, I decided to sneak and use my phone to ask my friends to lunch after class. This time I wasn't being cautious, because she'd caught me and threatened that my phone would be taken away if she saw it out again. As she was threatening me, I quickly completed the class project as if I wasn't doing anything wrong. I knew I'd gotten caught, but if I could prove to her that I was working on the class project, I figured she would leave me alone. As soon as she turned her back to help another student, I got back on my cell phone. I kept my phone in my lap, so it wouldn't be confiscated if I got caught being on it again.

After completing the project, it was about time for dismissal, and my cell phone started vibrating repeatedly. I assumed that my friends were released early for class and that they had decided to go to lunch with me, but I couldn't look down to see who was texting me, because my teacher would have taken my phone. When I was finally able to check my phone, I saw a message from my oldest brother stating, "Pop just passed away."

I didn't know how to react, because I wasn't supposed to be on my phone. However, I couldn't hold back the grief and the pain that I felt going through my chest. I pushed back from the table and fell between my legs in tears. My classmates didn't know what had happened, but through my tears and screams, I overheard the teacher telling me to come into her office. When I got there, she told me that I needed to calm down and tell her what was going on. I didn't know how to state how I was feeling, and I didn't want to believe that it was true, so I called Mama instead.

While dialing her number, a part of me questioned myself, wondering why I'd even decided to call her, because she wasn't related to Pop. The other part of me thought it was the right thing to do, because she was the only person I truly trusted, and she knew what to say to help me get through that moment. On the call, I could tell that she hadn't gotten the news of Pop's passing, which was something I should have known prior to calling because she relied on me to tell her everything that was going on with my biological family.

After telling her the news, she apologized and told me that she would pick me up from school and take me over to my biological mother's house, where I wanted to be. Pop was her backbone, so now that he had died, she had no one to be there for her and to put up with her like her husband had. In the car on the way to the house, I was shaking in disbelief over his unexpected death. I was most concerned for my mother and little sister. I knew Pop was all they had, and I feared my mother would lose her mind and go back to her old ways of drug and alcohol addiction. Mama encouraged me by saying, "They'll be okay. God makes no mistakes." But I was certain that God had made a big mistake, because everyone knew that my little sister wouldn't have even been under the care of our mother had it not been for Pop.

When we arrived at the house, I jumped out the car and ran inside to comfort my mother and sister, who at the time was seven years old. Mama came in to give her sympathy, and she told me to let her know if we needed anything. I didn't want her to leave and go back to work, but I knew she wanted us to have some alone time. She always believed in us spending time with our biological family. After she left, some of my other siblings who had arrived before me, and our mother's close friends and Pop's family members waited quietly until our mother informed us of what had happened to him that led to his death. He had woken up and was preparing to take his medication as he left the bathroom. When he opened the door, he started yelling and pointing to his chest. He'd had a heart attack. She called nine-one-one to rush him to the hospital, but when the paramedics arrived, he had already gained his heavenly wings.

By dinner time, many family members and friends had heard about his death and started coming over to the house; they prayed for us and dropped off dishes of food. Freddie-Mae, my mother, told us to not eat certain foods, because she didn't trust the person's cooking; we laughed so hard, which brought back memories of how humorous Pop was when it came to food, because he wouldn't eat anybody's cooking except his wife's. Mama called for me later that night, asking if I was coming home or staying over. I wanted to go home and be with her, but I knew I needed to stay with my biological family, because this was the closest, we'd ever gotten to each other as a family.

Throughout the following week, we took care of the funeral arrangements. Before we allowed his body to be viewed by community members, we went to see him to make sure everything was good to go. Each of us hugged him and said our final farewells, because we wouldn't have much time during the funeral processional.

The day of the funeral, we woke up early and prayed as a family for strength before getting ready. The funeral home staff with the family limousines, so we could be on time for the program. When we arrived at the church, there were cars everywhere. The police department had to direct the flow of traffic, and a crossing guard guided the funeral attendees. So many people were impacted by him and thought it right to pay him respect, which was the best feeling for me. The funeral service and the repast went by smoothly. Afterwards, we departed and went our separate ways.

My mother went downhill from there. The grief from Pop's death overwhelmed her and took over her sense of thought. She started drinking every night and being physically and verbally abusive to anyone that came around, including our little sister who lived with her. She thought the taste of liquor and her drunk characteristics were solutions to the loss of the integral part of her life, Pop. Soon, the Department of Children and Families got involved and took the only child she had in her custody away. After a year of being in and out of the county jail, she got herself together and was able to get our sister back. I said a prayer.

August 2016

Dear Lord,

It's coming up to the fourth year of Pop's passing. I ask you to give my biological mother strength to do right. Out of all nine of her children, she only has one that she has been able to keep, so please allow her to get her act together and do what needs to be done. I don't know what her mindset is, but I know you are a healer. I ask for you to release all the pain she is still feeling from Pop's death. This is not the time for her to be reckless.

I also ask you to give me the endurance to bring my biological family closer together. Since Pop's funeral, all my brothers and sisters have been distant. It was my hope that my biological family stayed connected after the funeral because we need each other. We shouldn't have to wait until someone passes away to love and talk to each other. Mama always told me, "People would rather wait until you're dead and gone to bring you flowers than while you're living." I believe that was the exact predicament my family was in. We were divided by a system when we were younger, and now that we were of age to make our own decisions, no one had the time or energy to revive our family. We were so caught up in our own issues that we didn't have time to care for ourselves, much less, each other.

Lord, I know everything will be alright because you have the last say so, and I want to be in your will and not in your way.

Amen.

Two Peas in a Pod

Nancy, my favorite cousin, was knowledgeable, open minded, determined, and had a heart for the people. I met her when I was eight years of age. She seemed much older, acted as a big sister to me, but was my cousin through my adoptive family. She was from Haiti, but no one would know that unless she opened and told you, or if you heard her speaking on the phone to her biological family. She had been in the foster care system just as I had been. We had similar childhoods. She was not as open as I was about her experience in foster care, but I didn't care. I knew she was destined for success and that foster care wouldn't be a stopping point for either of us.

The day she first arrived; she had several large trash bags filled with her belongings. Mama thought it was best for her to get adjusted and comfortable before I went over to meet her at my Aunt's house next door— she kept foster children as Nancy. She had a short natural afro, khaki capris, and a pink and purple striped blouse on. Her outer appearance looked nice, but I knew her inner self wasn't. She barely held a conversation, let alone spoke, as she took her clothes and shoes out of the black garbage bags and put them in the compartments in her room and her closet. While still trying to hold a conversation with her, I heard Mama talking outside walking closer to the entrance of the door; this was my signal to leave before she got into me about aggravating Nancy.

It took a few weeks for her to get adjusted and accustomed to me wanting to hang out. Soon, we did almost everything together. Through elementary and middle school, we grew closer to one another, told each other secrets, and stayed to the wee hours of the morning talking about life and how beautiful it could be for us. As time went on, we came to a mutual understanding that no one around us understood our thoughts on success. We saw endless opportunities for ourselves if we worked hard and had faith. Others saw small obstacles as confirmation that they wouldn't amount to anything or be able to achieve their personal and professional goals. Those same people only worked to get by and to say that they had done something worthwhile with themselves, while Nancy and I worked for the opportunity to impact others around us. We were never average; in fact, we were convinced that we would be the example that everyone would follow, no matter the age or background. We learned from the failures and missed opportunities of others around us. Our only goal was to have a decent living, to not have to worry about finances because they would be in order, and to live happily. We didn't know how that would come about. if we had a plan and the will to get it done, it would be accomplished.

Education was essential for her. She was the nerd, making straight A's. I didn't care about perfect grades, I just wanted to pass to class. Nancy didn't like that mindset. Day in and day out she would encourage me to strive harder, tutored me with homework, and helped me study for upcoming exams. She believed that if we graduated grade school and went off to college to get a degree, we would be set for life. I started believing that too.

However, she didn't have to deal with all the family issues I had to deal. Her parents didn't live in United States, let alone in the same city as my biological family. Often time growing up she saw and heard the problems I faced with my biological family, so she understood why I wasn't mentally and emotionally strong like she was. There was no hiding anything from one another. Even if we tried, we would end up finding out. Despite living in two separate houses and being forced to believe in the saying, "What goes on in my house, stays in my house," we would still tell each other what was happening behind the closed doors of our homes and minds.

I was the vocal one of the pod; Nancy was the hardcore one. Wherever she went, people knew I would be right by her side or on my way to meet her. If I had an issue, Nancy would be there to handle it, just as I would be there for her. We didn't let our guards down for anyone, and no one could separate us, especially when in high school. Nancy was a grade higher than me, which was great. I was could get more insight and be more prepared for the transition for the next year or school. When I did get to high school, our bond became even stronger.

We didn't care about going out with friends or what others were doing; our minds were only focused on our futures—to ensure that we were well prepared. We were two individuals coming from two different backgrounds, enduring hardships and going through a foster care system that was equivalent to playing checkers with our lives. But we had a vision, goals, and different plans for achieving each goal. The goals that were set were very doable, we just had to stay focused.

Seven years after moved in with my auntie, she had not been offered the opportunity to be adopted. Many questions arose between Nancy, her my auntie, and Mama because by then, it didn't make sense why she hadn't been adopted. She and her foster mother rarely communicated about it. Nancy didn't want to create any tension between them. She planned to get a job soon to shop for herself In a few short years, she would be a legal adult and leaving for college. It hurt me to know she was a perfect child and still didn't have the opportunity to receive the benefits of being adopted and having a family that she could officially call hers.

Nancy's first real job was at Goodwill. I thought it was hilarious for her to be working there because she was the first person, I knew who worked for a company that sold hand-me-downs. It wasn't as if I didn't have used clothes in my drawer or closet–most of them were. But I thought she wouldn't want to be in that environment when we had the same clothes back home. But she wasn't thinking of where the clothes came from or who wore them. She thought about the lives she could impact through her contagious smile and personality.

When she came home from work, she'd always pop in and tell me about her shift; there was never a dull shift for her and never a time she came home without bags from shopping while working. If you asked me, I thought she was becoming a shopaholic. Every time she came home, she had something new. Sometimes, her items were under $1, even for name-brand clothing. When she told me her shopping techniques, I began shopping there as well. We shopped when she was at work, even on the days she wasn't scheduled to work. She taught me that broke people stayed broke because they constantly bought things they couldn't afford. I had fallen victim to these same bad shopping habits until she forced me to start being fiscally responsible.

After seeing how well she balanced work and school, I got the job at McDonald's. We didn't have a car at the time, so we rode the city bus together every day after school. While waiting on the bus near our school, we would stand under the tree and hide behind the tree trunk, so we wouldn't be seen by our friends or teachers; we were so embarrassed. Even though most of our friends had cars at the time, we would never ask if they would give us a ride, because we didn't like to depend on anyone for anything. Our mothers were still at work. They had already told us that if we got jobs, we'd be responsible for our own transportation, except for in the evenings when they could pick us up.

When it was time for us to get paid, we taught each other how to budget. We created our own checking and savings accounts with the banks we thought had the most benefits based on our independent research. We hoped we wouldn't have to go into our account unless it was an emergency, since we did have our families. That hope didn't last long, because both of our families believed that once you start making your own money you must start taking care of yourself. When our families would ask us for money, we either pretended like we didn't have it, or we would help them out based on the circumstance. It took a lot for either one of us to say yes, because we knew that our families weren't financially fit, because they weren't taught how to be. Though we weren't educated ourselves, we didn't want our money to run out.

Our families weren't accustomed to saving money living paycheck to paycheck. We always encouraged them to not spend their money frivolously and to pay their bills first. Even then, I believed it was financially irresponsible to not have multiple sources of income; however, both of our moms believed the best route was to work for the state, retire, and live off retirement funds and social security checks. Nancy and I didn't think that was sustainable.

Throughout our times together, Nancy and I were encouraged to stay on the right track, especially when we saw some of our closest relatives struggling daily. We wanted more for them, but we knew we couldn't give them what they needed; they had to work just as hard as we were working. They tried but fear held them back. Nancy and I knew that we didn't want to live the lifestyles they were living. Not that their lifestyles were bad, but we just wanted more for ourselves and to make better decisions that would affect us positively for years to come.

We both knew that when people didn't have money, the entire atmosphere would change for them. From on-going complaints, to cracking down on how much food we could eat, to hearing the change jar being shaken up to see if they could scrape up enough silver coins to make a dollar or two. Nancy's foster mother had it the worst. If she didn't have any money, she made it known through her silence. Her facial expressions spoke for her. She would go days without mumbling a word, and if she did it wasn't much. She would stay in her bed all day and watch television and wouldn't cook, or smoke cigarettes throughout the day. We never could understand how she was able to find money to purchase a pack of Benson and Hodges 100 Menthol Lights. She could have saved money to go towards things that she needed that would ultimately get her back to her happy place financially. Nancy thought her foster mom was depressed by her actions when her money was low.

Mama would just complain to Peanut and me that she is a single mother, barely making any money, and that the monthly stipends she would get for us didn't help with anything since it wasn't much of nothing. She too, would go next door to her sister house to get some cigarettes, or send me over there to get them for her so her nerves could calm down-though I knew that they would only be calmed down for a few moments. Right when the cigarette taste went away, she would still be in the same predicament: financially stressed. Any time these episodes occurred, Nancy and I only would tell each other "This could have been prevented had both of our parents listened to us."

Nancy's foster mom had an addiction to smoking cigarettes. One afternoon after school, Nancy and I didn't have work, so we went on the school bus to go home. After walking home, Nancy called me over to see the cigarettes in her mother's bathroom she'd recently had added on to their house. The bathroom design was nice but couldn't hide the leftover yellow stains on the blinds or the ashes from all the cigarettes in the ashtray that she'd hid in the drawer. Nancy would get upset and complain about her mother's addiction to cigarettes, because she couldn't afford to smoke them and pay all her bills on time, not to mention the many health effects associated with smoking. I knew exactly where she was coming from, because Mama smoked occasionally but would try to hide it from us. When I found out, I threw the pack of cigarettes in the trash, but she would end up going back to the store to buy more.

When we realized that educating them on the effects of smoking wasn't working, we hoped commercials would do the trick. Nancy always tried to hold her laughter in because she didn't want to seem rude; I, on the other hand, turned the volume up and recited the entire commercial, so they knew that it was a serious matter.

Nancy and I rarely got a chance to hang out with friends, and the times we did were a challenge if we were dependent on her mother taking us to our friends' house. When we got permission to stay the weekend at one of our friends', there was always an issue with gas. Her tank was always empty, and she'd always ask us for gas money in exchange for taking us places. She would pull into the gas station and not say a word. She didn't even take off her seat belt or look in our direction. We thought it was the funniest thing ever. As she sat there in silence, so did we. After a few minutes, Nancy's Foster Mother would turn to us and say, "I'll turn this car back around and carry both of you home. Maybe then you'll be able to find someone else to take you." We didn't have a choice but to pay for the gas, and then we were on our way. We cherished every moment we could away from home, because outside of our homes we were in different environments with people we loved who we knew were trying to do great things in their lives as well.

God always had something special in store for the both of us, even when it seemed as if things were against us. The day Nancy left to attend The University of West Florida, we agreed that we wouldn't go without talking to each other, no matter how far we went in life.

THE INTERNSHIP

While I was working for McDonald's, I knew that flipping burgers and coming home late at night smelling like fried food wouldn't be my lifetime career. What I didn't know was that I would have the opportunity to see early on what my career might look like by gaining an internship.

After completing all the requirements to graduate high school a year early, l, I was focused on spending time with my family, friends and girlfriend, Sharinse before going off to college at Bethune-Cookman University. Though I spent most of my time with my girlfriend—because we worked together and spent time together when we were off—I was battling with my sexuality. She knew it but didn't know how to say it because I told her I was straight and had good intentions.

While at home, I'd watch Law & Order, Criminal Minds, and court shows. My interest in getting involved with the law sparked even more after the Trayvon Martin shooting in February of 2012 in Sanford, Florida. Racial inequality in the criminal justice system led me to seek an internship with the attorney who'd represented the fallen teen, Benjamin Crump. Crump operated a law firm with his partner, Daryl Parks, which was about fifteen minutes away from my house.

Two weeks before my high school graduation, I went on the Parks & Crump LLC website to find internship opportunities. As none were showcased on the site, I came up with my own conclusion that the firm had ceased their internship program due to the high exposure the office acquired during the Trayvon Martin trial. So, I went back to YouTube to listen to the trial and study all the attorneys who'd taken part in the case. I found myself rewinding the videos, searching for tone, facial gestures, hidden signals—any tricks and techniques that were displayed throughout the cross examination, and so on.

Nearly a year after the trial, I still had not found a way to join the firm. I found myself making excuses, like preparing to graduate high school, gearing up for college, hanging out with friends when I had the time—anything but moving toward my goal. I figured that the firm was playing catch up on other clients and initiatives and too busy to look at interns.

The Friday after graduation, Mama wanted to take her grand-kids and foster children to a newly renovated Cascades Park. The kids wanted to play in the imagination fountain and see the nighttime light. I was excited about going with them, because it would be my first time seeing the new renovations since it's re-opening.

The day of the outing, I told Mama that we would drive separate cars. She asked why, as I knew she would since we were going to be bonding all day. I didn't want to ride with her, because I knew how aggravating it was to ride with the kids. If I was going to spend a full day with them at a park, I had to mentally prepare myself. I couldn't tell her that, though. Instead, I told her that I needed to go see my biological mother first, which was a lie. The truth is, I didn't have any additional plans, but to make me feel better about the situation, I stopped by my job to get a free meal.

It was about one thirty in the afternoon when I left my job to head to Cascades Park. As I turned out of the McDonald's parking lot, a commercial came on the radio that highlighted Attorney Benjamin Crump's services and accomplishments. How ironic, I thought. From that commercial, two thoughts came to mind: Go back home and email someone at the law firm and pray that they would respond. Or, I could just walk in and see if I could talk to someone.

I drove to the law firm and walked inside. As I approached the door, I started getting nervous, because I knew I didn't have an appointment and I wasn't a client. However, I walked in with my loafers, jeans, and polo shirt and was greeted by the law clerk who sat in the atrium of the firm.

Immediately, she asked, "Do you have an appointment with someone in this office today?" I had to come up with a reason for my visit, which would persuade her to get someone to speak to me about the opportunity to intern with them. I stared at her and looked down as if I didn't know what to say—she was intimidating. She then excused herself for a few moments and left the room. Seconds later, a man walked up and asked, "How can I help you?"

I was finally able to proceed with my answer. "I would like to know if I can be an intern for this office?"

He looked at me then back at the clerk and told me to follow him to the conference room. That was my confirmation that I had my foot in the door. Now it was up to me to seal the deal. That was the easy part.

He continued asking questions, and even though I didn't have an educated response for all of them, I persuaded him enough to bring me on as an intern starting that upcoming Monday. I was excited but, on the inside, I didn't think I was ready. They were only accustomed to hiring interns who were either obtaining their bachelor's degree or who were already in law school. However, I didn't allow it to dissuade me.

After we said our farewells, I immediately went to the park with my family to tell them about the opportunity I'd just received. They couldn't believe it. My mama was proud of me, so we went to dinner after the light show to celebrate. Over the weekend, I ironed the hand-me-down suits and ties that Mama had gotten for me from a deacon at the church. When Monday morning came, I felt sick on the inside, because I really didn't know what I had gotten myself into. But I was going to get through it, because I knew that I hadn't come this far to give up.

There wasn't a day in the office that was the same as the one before. Each day, I received different assignments: preparing reports for court hearings, filing and pulling files from the archives, interviewing clients, sitting in meetings and taking notes, and, the most difficult task for me, creating mailers. I read the instructions verbatim, but the mailers still did not come out right. Those were the only deadlines I ever missed.

I would leave my area and close Crump's office door as he was working on reports on the computer, so he wouldn't see me trying to figure out the machine that printed them out. I would get frustrated and start going around the office seeing if any of the other attorneys or staff needed me to do anything. If anyone else had something for me to do, I would do it, so by the time my supervisor requested to see the mailers, I would have an excuse as to why I couldn't complete them. Soon, he realized that I didn't know how to complete the task and assured me that they didn't expect me to know how to do everything. He went on to tell me that I was hired so that I could learn and grow my skills so that when it was time for me to practice law or work in the industry that best fit me, I could be prepared. I knew that I'd made the right decision in interning with this law farm.

One of the most interesting cases that I was able to take part in was the death of Kendrick Johnson, the black man whose body was found in a wrestling mat in the gymnasium of Lowndes High School in Valdosta, Georgia. Attorney Crump, my supervisor, and I sat down with the family. I was given the task of taking notes during the meeting. I had never taken legal minutes before, so I just did as my supervisor said. "Don't stop writing! Write down any and everything, especially the questions and responses that you will hear."

From the beginning of the meeting to the end, I had written down just about all the words that came out of everyone's mouths. I was determined not to mess up this assignment since I would have to type out all the notes and submit them to Attorney Crump before the end of the day.

There wasn't a specific time for lunch on any given day. You had to get lunch in between completing and starting a new project, or if there was a conference call taking place, you had to multitask between driving to the restaurant, talking on the phone with the client, and taking notes, while debating on where to eat. We had a McDonald's, Burger King, and Krispy Kreme in the area. If we were tired of fast food, we'd pre-order food, and I would pick it up for everyone.

When the bosses were in—Attorney Benjamin Crump or Attorney Daryl Parks—everyone in the office would wait until either of them was ready to eat. That way, we wouldn't have to spend money on lunch. We were spoiled. We could order anything we wanted, and one of them would foot the bill. When I first started my internship, I didn't know any better, so anytime either of the bosses asked me if I wanted anything to eat, I'd decline. I didn't want to spend money on lunch, and I didn't know that when a boss offers lunch, they mean that they will pay for it as well. Once I discovered that, I ordered lunch every time the boss asked. Sometimes I wasn't even hungry. However, I knew I couldn't say no, especially after seeing the other attorneys and staff ordering food. So, I'd just save it for dinner.

Though the internship wasn't paid, I still get reimbursed through the experiences and opportunities that were provided to me. One of those experiences was attending the National Bar Association Convention, hosted at the Marriott Marquis in downtown Atlanta. This convention year would be different for the law firm, because Attorney Crump was up to run for the 2015-2016 President of the organization. This organization is the oldest and largest voluntary professional membership organization for African American attorneys and judges which has more than 20,000 members. As the intern for that summer, I was busy assisting with the planning, organization and execution of the campaign events being held throughout the convention so that his coined slogan for the election "Preserving Our Past and Protecting Our Future" was heard and known at every event. I had not been on anyone's campaign in the past, so I learned a lot. Every meeting or conference call that I could join with the team, I made sure to be a part of. It was exciting to see Ben's vision come, and I wanted to be a vital part of that history. A week out from the convention, names were not solidified as to who would be attending or staying back at the firm. The team knew that they could get me to do all the running around if it got busy at the campaign site, so eventually I was informed that I could go. I went home and shared the news with Mama; she was excited! The morning of our departure, Mama came with me, so she could say her farewells and to speak with Attorney Crump. I didn't know what she'd be saying, but I knew she could be overprotective. She told him to take good care of me then went on and on, even giving him permission to whoop me if I got out of hand. At that point, I wanted to escort her out of the firm myself. She was doing the most for no reason.

Finally, she left, and shortly afterwards we packed the black Suburban with our luggage and campaign items and hit the road to Atlanta, Georgia. There were no breaks taken on the road to Atlanta. It got to the point where everyone except me was on a conference call. I was constantly moving my phone from window to window, trying to find service to get on the internet.

When we made it to the hotel, I shared a room with my supervisor because all the rooms were booked. I was not thought of when they originally booked hotel rooms months before I became an intern. I took my shower, ordered room service, and was out for the night. The next morning, the convention started, and though we wanted to have fun and enjoy other events, we were there for business only. We all met in a private room to discuss the staffing plan for that day. I was mostly stationed at the campaign table. On other days, I'd go to a session or two and listen to the different legal professionals speak on various topics. On the third day, I went to Phaedra Parks' *Secret of the Southern Belle* book signing. I didn't know anything about the book, but because she was on the Atlanta Housewives show, I felt the need to meet her. She was so down to earth and surprised that I was at the convention at to my age.

As Election Day got closer, we spent many nights staying up preparing for the next day or attending parties that one of the attorneys had in the hotel. I was most shocked to see attorneys and judges drunk, especially because I didn't think they had time to indulge in those types of activities. However, it was refreshing to know that they still were able to be themselves and be comfortable. The next night, we had to put door hangers on each of the doors in the hotel. We debated for a long time on the time we should meet up, because we knew the parties wouldn't end until about two in the morning. We all agreed to meet at two forty-five to complete the last big task before Election Day. To my surprise, many people were still up, so some of the convention registrants were rude, telling me to leave from their doors and that Ben Crump didn't deserve to win. I assumed it was because they knew I was on Attorney Crump's campaign team, and they were not planning to vote for him— my supervisor said that's the way politics are and that I would have to get used to it. Once I finished my stack around four a.m., I went back to my room, showered, watched CNN and fell asleep.

On Election Day, all of Attorney Crump's staff and campaign supporters had on his official campaign shirt. We had signs, posters, and literature pamphlets throughout the campaign site, so that anyone who wanted to be part of the team, would have items to help spread the word about the campaign. The other candidate's team had the same, however, we were a bit more professional. With our large volunteer team, we all split up and groups and manned the entire convention center. Our strategy enabled us to meet, connect and influence convention registrants who had no clue to who to vote for. We wanted to ensure that everyone knew the name Ben Crump when it was time to cast their vote. Though we already knew that everyone knew his name and face from previous trials, we still gave all we had. We knew that he would win the seat if we did our jobs right, so we stayed on our Ps and Qs.

When voting was over, we shut down our voting table and went to dinner to celebrate the pre-victory. We knew that we had the election without a doubt because most voters left the voting room cheering for Ben Crump! Later, we were informed that Attorney Benjamin Crump had gotten seventy-two percent of the vote-a landslide. To end the convention and celebrate our win, we had another party and invited everyone to attend.

I decided to leave the party early to go to a musical at the Gospel Music Workshop of America, Inc., Sunday Best Season 3 Winner, Le'Andria Johnson, was set to perform next door at the Hyatt. I didn't have tickets, but I managed to get in free with seats in the front row. I sent a text message to Le'Andria's manager after receiving his number at a concert that she was performing in Tallahassee months previously. He met me at the entry of the concert and told security that I was part of Le'Andria's team. After the concert, I went bac to my hotel, ordered food room service, and went fast asleep. The next morning, we headed back to Tallahassee.

THE NEVER-ENDING FAMILY

A foster home is one where you're destined to experience multiple emotions and perspectives, a home where the government has the ultimate say so and full control over what goes on between those walls. It's a home that's said to be temporary housing for children who cannot stay with their biological parents for a range of reasons: sexual abuse, physical abuse, emotional abuse, exploitation, domestic violence, parental absence, parental incapacity, parental substance/alcohol abuse, medical neglect, or even the failure to thrive. The house that I had the privilege to call home, Mama's house, had kept more than one hundred different foster children. It was a house that taught me to understand that each day brought about a different result, and it was up to me to make it a home for all the broken hearts that entered those doors. I did this by opening sharing my story of growing up being in foster care and sharing the things that made them feel at home; PlayStation, bike, and let them have some of my clothes and shoes if they didn't have much.

This experience was one worth living. Mama had been taking in children since before she took me in, since before I was even born. She wasn't new to this; she knew what was necessary to make a child feel welcomed and loved. When one walked through the doors with their black garbage bags filled with clothes, she wouldn't let those bags enter any bedrooms. She was disgusted that the placement staff had the audacity to bring all that the child had in black bags, as if it was trash. Moments later, you would hear the washer and dryer running so all the clothes would be clean and smell fresh.

Before nighttime, the holy oil was prayed over, and she touched every doorknob and wall in the house. She didn't want bad spirits to enter the house, because it was her responsibility to ensure that each child was safe and secure. It didn't matter the reasoning behind the placement; her job was to help once that child stepped into her house.

When a child is placed in the foster care system, they must deal with many people, whether they want to or not. These people can include birth family, attorneys, placement staff, social workers, therapists, law enforcement, and the independent living case manager. Mama knew how overwhelming it could be, so she did her best to create a positive environment for the child and informed them of ways she could help them achieve their dreams even when they returned to their biological parents.

One of my foster brothers, Carlos, was nine years old. He was tall, plump, had large eyes, and loved to eat. Every time you looked up; he was eating something. Peanut and I didn't understand what he was going through. Mama always had food, but he ate like food was scarce. Months later, he finally understood that our house wouldn't run out of food, so he didn't have to worry about going hungry. He was able to adapt to the house comfortably. His sister was placed next door at my auntie's

After staying with us for three years, he found out that he couldn't go back with his mother, who wasn't following her case plan. His case worker asked if he wanted to continue staying with us, or if he wanted to try a new foster home. Carlos asked to stay with us as he liked where he was at, and he didn't want to have to get adjusted to a new foster family.

We were close in age and faced puberty around the same time. Some days we would get along, and other days we were at each other's throats.

I truly cared for him, because I was once in his shoes, but I wasn't going to allow him to talk to me any kind of way and let him continue getting me in trouble for his mistakes. I would make him upset by mimicking him and laughing when he didn't understand something. I would feel bad and try to fix the situation because I didn't like to be mimicked or laughed at. I wasn't being serious. He was very emotional and took everything to the heart.

Mama would hear him and I bickering back and forth and yell, "I don't even know why you all are being like that to each other; you live in the same house, eat the same food, wash your ass in the same tub; so, if anything, you should be looking out for each other and loving each other as real brothers." We both knew she was telling the truth, so we would apologize and be friends…until another issue sparked an argument. I felt like I was right about everything since I'd lived in the house longer than him. I wasn't always right, and if I was, I still knew it was wrong for me to laugh and argue with him just for fun.

Two years later, we both wanted a fish tank, so we put our monthly allowance together to purchase the items for the tank. We spent countless hours in Walmart selecting a tank, fish and the decorations we wanted to go in the tank. After we went home to set it up, we made a feeding schedule, so Mama could see that we were working together. Two weeks after installing the tank, I came home from school and all the fish were floating upside down, dead. He had overfed the fish. Fish food was scattered across the floor and floating in the water. I was livid. I didn't want to share a fish tank with him anymore, so I decided to go get my own tank, fish and decorations. When I came home for the second time in a row, my fish were dead. This time, he'd poured bleach in the tank, because he was upset that I went and got another tank. There were no more fish in the house after that day. Mama wasn't upset that the fish died—she was more upset that he used bleach to kill them.

During Christmas time, Mama got a call from the placement office regarding a six-year-old Hispanic boy who needed temporary care. Mama was prone to keeping children within our race, but she knew that any time she could get called to keep children of different races—it was up to her to decide if she was going to. She asked the placement staff to give her a few minutes, put her on mute and called for Peanut, Carlos, and I to ask our opinion because we were all set for Christmas. We thought it would be a good idea for her to take him in since it was the holidays and we knew that if we were in his shoes we would want to be with a family for holidays—even if it wasn't our own biological family. She un-muted the call and told the placement staff that she would keep him. An hour later the placement staff dropped him off with his clothes in the black bag. From the time he stepped inside our home, he cried for hours asking if he could go back to his Mom. We went through this several times over the years, so we knew that the crying would eventually stop once he knew he was in good hands.

Mama went to wrap her arms around him to give him more comfort, and to let him know that she will do everything that she can to make him feel like he's home. Usually, that would calm the child down, but this time; that method didn't work. Moments later, the little boy started throwing picture frames from the living room table, end tables and wall mount, breaking them. He then started taking his anger out by kicking the walls in the house. Mama was scared, so had us to run into her bedroom and close the door until he calmed down. It was almost midnight, and Mama didn't want to call the placement staff, so she left her bedroom once we didn't hear any noise or him crying to talk to him. She wasn't upset about the glass being broken; she was more concerned about him hurting himself because of how hurt he was from the separation. Mama wanted to be sure that he wouldn't have any more episodes that night, so she took him to his favorite fast-food restaurant, McDonald's to get a happy meal—which calmed him down, and by the time they pulled up in the driveway, he was fast asleep. Mama carried him into his bedroom, the one that had Sponge Bob theme so he could remain asleep for the night.

The next morning, Mama called the placement staff to inquire if the kid had any issues, because she had never experienced anything like that. Placement came out to talk to the kid and told him that he couldn't destroy the property. He promised that he wouldn't, however, when it was time for him to go to bed that night, he started destroying our things once more. This time, he was kicking the ornaments off the tree and throwing them at the walls. He kicked the gifts and made the entire Christmas tree fall, which made Mama very upset because she had recently replaced the carpet with laminated wood in the living room, and she was afraid that the water from the Christmas tree stand would swell up her floor. After he wrecked the inside decorations, he went outside and started taking the lighted candy-canes out of the grown and kicking the inflated Santa Clause Mama immediately called the placement staff and informed them that they needed to place him in another home as soon as possible. By the time they arrived to pick him up, his clothes were packed up. After he left, we re-decorated the tree, and put up the decorations outside.

The day before Christmas Eve, Mama began to feel bad that she made the placement staff pick him-up. She worried nobody would want to keep him temporarily, so she decided to give him another shot, believing she had solved the method to his madness.

When she called the placement staff to request that they bring him back—which they agreed to because he was in a group home with other children-- she sat down with Carlos and the caseworker. She explained to him that she's there to help, and that she loves him just as she loves her other children. She went on to tell him that Santa Clause wanted to meet him that evening, so he had to be good while he was staying there to get gifts on Christmas Day.

Since that talk, he got better each day. After weeks of understanding and adjusting to his ways, he started listening more and he understood that all Mama wanted to do was care for him until he was placed back with his family. As foster children continued coming in and out of the house, I knew that their lives were being impacted positively, and that Mama was sowing good seeds into them. Her taking in more children and keeping them temporarily allowed Peanut and I to remain humble and understand that there are many children in the foster system who need just as much attention as we needed when we first arrived at Mama's house. She has a big heart, especially for vulnerable children.

MIRROR, MIRROR

Waking up every morning is a blessing that I will never take for granted. On most mornings I find myself staring at the bathroom mirror, trying to figure out how I've made it this far in life. I'm sure that everyone takes a moment sometimes to wonder the same thing. Although, I wish I didn't have to face the hardships I did and I am not blinded by the fact that they won't still come throughout my life.; Still, I know I was built for this life. I made up in my mind years ago that I will be prepared for what's to come. My well-preparedness causes questions of curiosity from outsiders, and when I am asked, "What would you like to be when you grow up?" I always answer their question with a question.

"How can you determine if one has grown up or not?"

In my time of living, I've concluded that one's growth is dependent on his own self. Some people just don't want to grow up and be better, and then we have those who will work until their vision becomes a reality. In today's world, people have been taught that when they turn eighteen years of age, they are considered grown. I defy that. Every family has a cousin, brother, sister, auntie, or uncle who by law is considered a legal adult, but by nature is still a child within. There are also some families that have someone who is by law not considered a legal adult but is somehow doing much better than their older relatives, thus proving the notion that age is simply a number. You can be old and have been afforded the same opportunities as someone younger yet decided not to embrace the opportunity to the fullest. Sometimes, this can lead to bitterness about one's life accomplishments.

I believe that not all people grow up, and some of those people complain excessively. Even when everything is going right, they will find something to complain about. It is annoying, and disruptive to my focused mindset. Many of us find more negative issues rather than looking at the positives, which causes us to fall into depression and procrastinate. This is typically why most aren't successful. When you begin to look at where you were versus where you are now, I am sure you can say that things have improved. Even if you are not where you intended to be at this day and time, use the time now as preparation for your next level. I believe that time is the currency of the Earth. Though you cannot survive without having money, you can always get it back, but time, you can't. I'd rather have someone take my money than to take my time, because I can make up money, but I can't make up time.

I knew I could experience something different if I put myself in a position to do so. I was shy and afraid every time I thought about relocating after high school graduation. Being under Mama growing up made me that way. I was afraid of the home cooked meals I would miss, the conversations and events, but there was one thing that I was certain of: I wasn't going to let anything, or anyone rob me of my future. I knew something greater was inside of me.

Each night before going to sleep, I researched people's locations and success stories. I tried to compare their lives to mine, then started believing that relocating would free my mind from all the issues that life threw at me in my hometown. Or, possibly, moving might put me in a different environment, forcing me to grow in ways I didn't think I could.

I told myself, "If I think positive, I will reap positive. If I think negative, I will reap negative." It's easier said than done, but when I started to know who I was and whose I was, I was able to look back in that mirror at myself and tell myself, "Boy, you can make it."

Once upon a time I believed my past defined who I was and who I was going to be. At one point, I thought there was a curse over my biological family. My oldest sister and brother were complacent, my biological mother was in and out of jail and could never keep a job, and Peanut no longer cared about meeting goals and being successful. Furthermore, between both my biological and adoptive family, no one took their financial credit seriously, and they couldn't manage their funds correctly, so I figured that would be me as well. After a while, I made myself believe that since I wasn't surrounded by success or people that could manage the very things that made them happy, that I would be the same way since that was all I knew. Now, my view on success and "making it" is completely different. I believe that you are who you believe you are, and the power to achieve goals is in the power of your tongue, your ability to work toward it, and faith.

In my Understanding Faith class at Bethune-Cookman really understood what faith was about. Though it is the substance of things hoped for, and the evidence of things unseen, faith doesn't look at what you don't have, nor does it look at your circumstances. Faith is the ability to keep moving forward when it seems as if everything is against you.

Sometimes we don't believe in ourselves, or who we really can be, if we put in the work. We often forget that we're equipped with all the tools needed to get to the next level. The resources are there as well. The issue is, we don't always like to push ourselves more. Instead, we hinder ourselves by thinking about all the negative components, and everything that is going on in our family, and world. Though I am certain, if you take a few seconds to think about how far you really have come, you wouldn't talk yourself down, or beat yourself up. Everything you do starts with the mind. What you think you become. You must see things that are not as though they were.

SHARP EYE

I am not who I am because of my name. I am who I am today because of my hard work ethic. My name was given to me; my accomplishments are the testament of my earnings that I worked hard to receive. I was a student at Bethune-Cookman University, a Historically Black College and University (HBCU). Founded on what was once a city dump site. The university was started with just one dollar and fifty cents, five little girls, and faith in God by a woman named Dr. Mary McLeod Bethune.

Before I committed to attend this university, the University of North Florida was one of my top undergraduate choices as well. However, the hospitality, students, and staff at Bethune took my heart. I'm glad I went an alternate route; I don't think I'd be as happy and as determined as I am today if I hadn't.

I was so caught up on ensuring that my grades were perfect while in college, I never thought of joining any organizations. Then, I received a call from DaQuan Bryant, the current Student Government Association President requesting me to be at an upcoming student body meeting. I didn't believe in myself at that time, because I didn't think I was able to fulfill any duties and responsibilities that would be given to me. However, I came out on top. After a while, many administrators, faculty, staff, and students on the campus knew who I was and the work that I completed from attending meetings to help representing the student body, to speaking on behalf of the university at events in the community and being personal and relatable events to my colleagues. By my junior year, I was elected as the Student Body President, a position that I didn't take lightly. I used my platform to cultivate the students and lead the university to a promising future through my campaign slogan "A New Day at B-CU."

If I don't take anything else from this experience, I will take the gift of networking and developing meaningful relationships. I never had the opportunity to meet and surround myself with successful people before college. But now that I have, I've made it my priority to take full advantage of the opportunities provided by my colleagues and the staff at Bethune. I realize that it isn't always about what you know but who you know.

Three months into my reign, I received an email from the University President. In the email was an invitation requesting my attendance at the Vince Carter Charity Gala, a gala that would honor key people within the Daytona Beach community that contributed greatly to higher education. As I continued reading through the invitation, I thought the email was mistakenly sent to me, because I didn't know any of the honorees, and there was going to be alcohol at the event. Typically, any event that I've attended hasn't offered alcohol, because students would be in attendance, and according to the University policy, students could not attend events that offered alcohol, no matter the age of the student.

Days went by, and I hadn't decided on whether I would be in attendance. The next morning before class, I received an automatic reminder email that gave me more details on the event. I didn't open the email at first because I was finishing up a project for my International Studies Course—a project that I had put off for months. After class, I checked my email and realized that the deadline had passed to confirm my attendance. I made the decision not to attend the gala, especially since I didn't have anything to wear.

At that same time, I remembered Mama saying, "Don't leave outside the house door knowing you're not representing the brand of being one of my boys. The people already think black males aren't worth a dime, so anytime you get an opportunity, go for it because that may be the very thing that will take you up."

I went back to the email to re-read the invitation once more. Moments later, I received a call from my College English I professor, who always believed that I would be well-known all over the world my first day in her course. From the way I dressed (during that time hand-me down suits and ties from the deacons from my church back home), and my motivational speeches that I gave the class throughout the semester she knew I would touch the lives of many people. I was shocked when she said, "I am anticipating your presence at the gala tonight,

I didn't want to tell him that I wasn't interested in going, so I stated, "I'm busy now," and we said our farewells and hung up.

Immediately after hanging up with him, I got a second call, this time from one of the officers on my executive board. "Do you have anyone going with you to the gala, because if not, I would like to ride with you." I was quiet for a couple seconds because it seemed as if many people were expecting my attendance. I told him I would get right back to him. I went downstairs to the lobby to get a Snickers bar out of the vending machine. I couldn't believe that so many people were expecting me to go to this thing. Afterwards, I went back to my room and devoured the bar in seconds. Later, my stomach felt like it was flipping, so I decided to lie down, hoping the pain would ease up. I dozed off for a few minutes then jumped up as soon as I realized that the gala would be starting soon, and I started getting excited about it. I got dressed fast and headed to the gala. The whole time while getting ready, I tried to talk myself out of going because I started getting butterflies in my stomach—but I pushed through it. As I left campus, two students stopped me and asked to ride with me so we could split the cost of parking. Upon arriving, we saw many people having their cars valeted. They were getting out of nice cars. Every time someone pulled up, we would whoop and holler and say, "That's going to be my ride one day!"

I was still grateful for my car, because I had recently gotten a new one, but I knew it wasn't that much of a luxury, because the manufacturer of my car had stopped making my model years ago. However, I parked very sophisticatedly, and we got out and walked toward the main entrance of the event. As we entered the atrium, there were abstract paintings posted along the entrance of the ballroom. There were security officers and a doorkeeper, ensuring only credentialed people were allowed into the event.

After waiting in line at the check-in table that was draped in a silky lavender tablecloth with diamond centerpieces, I was informed that my ticket was already taken care of through my University President; and that my table and server were waiting for me. The greeter provided me with my table number and a seating chart- I was shocked! I wasn't sitting in the back as I thought I would be since I was student. Instead, I was sitting directly across from the stage right by the head table, front and center.

When we entered the banquet room, we could hear a live band playing soft classical music. All the women were wearing nice, elegant gowns. The men wore tailored suits with different designer socks, and it looked as if they had just gotten their shoes shined. From one wall to the next, tables were filled with nice, expensive items that were being auctioned off and all monies raised would go towards the Embassy of Hope. Most of the bidders looked like they had big money with the way they dressed in their designer clothes, shoes, and fancy jewelry.

There were high-quality food baskets for auction, diamond and gold necklaces, brackets, anklets and watches, vacation packages to destinations I had never even heard of. From that moment, I knew we were among people with real coins. Sitting down at my table, I received hospitality better than Chick-Fil-A. My waitress didn't want us to do anything but have a good time! We were told that there was plenty of alcohol, and all that we had to do was go order from the bar. It sounded good, but on the inside, I knew I wasn't legally able to drink any alcoholic beverages; therefore, I requested a Sprite with a hint of orange juice on the rocks to portray as if I had some liquor.

Before the program started, I went to the bathroom and cursed myself out. I couldn't believe I had almost let this opportunity go by. Had I not had the courage to come, I wouldn't have had this great experience. "Excuses are tools of the incompetent," I kept telling myself. I'm not incompetent; I am above and beyond all that anyone could ever think of me to be.

When I got back to my table, I mentioned to my friends that we were favored to be in attendance of such an upscale event. I knew that if it were not for me receiving those encouraging calls, I wouldn't have been at the gala. I had to understand that sometimes people in your life see things well before you see them, and it's during those times that you must trust their word and go for it.

Throughout the room, donors and sponsors sat eating at the auction tables or stood talking to their millionaire friends. a. My friends and I thought we had to wait to be served, but we were able to get up and get food if desired. So, we did. There was quiche, meatballs, crab cakes, grits and shrimp, baked bread, chicken kabobs, and more. I couldn't eat everything, but I tried. My eyes eventually got bigger than my stomach.

Walking around the room, I overheard several conversations about people giving millions of dollars to different charities throughout the country. I felt honored to be in the presence of such people. Moments later, I met a very powerful and well-known man, Vince Carter. Carter is an American professional basketball player for the Memphis Grizzlies of the National Basketball Association (NBA). He looked to be about six and a half feet tall and exuded confidence; his demeanor showed it all. He walked around the gala with his head held high. His handshakes were strong and firm. At first, I was afraid to ask him questions about his success, but I conquered my fears by talking with him for a few minutes. He did everything people told him he couldn't do. Before we parted, he told me to "keep the faith, and never give up."

Shortly after, more students surrounded him, listening to what he had to say. Our eyes were glued to him. We couldn't turn away from him for anything. We wanted to receive everything he was telling us so that when we left the event to go back to our residence halls, we could work on our own dreams. I gained so much knowledge from him within those few short minutes. I was astonished, but very grateful and humble. Going back to our seats, I found myself thumping my hand and pinching myself to make sure I wasn't dreaming. It had always been my wish to meet a man who that was successful. I was living out my dreams!

The host began recognizing special donors based off their level of commitment. I pulled out my pen and pad, so I could write down all the names that were being called. I wanted to look for them after the program and introduce myself. First impressions are what help you get your foot in the door. When it was time, I went around and spoke to all the people that were on my list. I first thanked each of them for their generous donations, then I told them about my student leadership experience on campus and my plans after graduation. As soon as we were done speaking, we traded business cards so that we could stay in contact after the gala.

It started getting late, so my friends and I agreed to leave. Deep down, I didn't want to leave, but I knew I would have more opportunities soon. On the way to my residence hall, I began thumping myself once more. I wasn't sure why I was so shocked when I dreamed for opportunities like this—to be in a room filled with hundreds of successful people leaving me with a lifetime of knowledge. One of the most valuable things I learned from this gala was the ability to network so that when I am ready for the next step, I have a team of people I can call on.

It was never my goal to be the richest person in the world—money is the root to all evil. I am still convinced that money can't take away emotional or mental illness. The Forbes list is something I wouldn't mind being on; however, that, too, isn't my goal in life. My goal is to gain all the knowledge possible that will equip me to bring about radical change in our world and to impact each life that I come across.

Mama would always say, "A man filled with knowledge is a man not worth losing."

THE NAVIGATOR

T he morning after the gala, I called and told Mama about the experience. Unfortunately, she didn't seem that excited for me, though I didn't allow it to bother me too much. I expected her to be jubilant, but instead she began questioning my ability to have good grades with such a busy social life. She believed that my grades were slipping because I wasn't attending class as much as she deemed necessary. Though she had a point, I knew the type of learner I was. I didn't need to attend class if I knew what was being lectured. I could simply read the course book and retain the knowledge, and if I didn't understand a concept, I knew I could always count on YouTube or Google to teach me the concept step-by-step.

Furthermore, we live in a world full of opportunities, and I wanted to use my days in college in a smart way, because undergraduate days swiftly pass by. After being around my mentors, leaders in the community, and hearing different success stories I realized that having just a degree wasn't going to get me where I wanted to be in life. On the other side, I also knew I didn't need confirmation from anyone about anything that I was doing. When you have complete control over your life, your "Personal Navigation for Success (PNS)," is ultimately up to you. This comes after taking your own calculated risks and doing what you, yourself, think is best for your future.

Nancy would always remind me, "Don't let nobody live their life through you." I never understood what she meant by that because I was young, dumb, and naïve. However, when I left for college, it came to me; people—whether they are family, friends or folks you don't even know—will try to live their lives through you. But I must remind them that there is nothing stopping them from living their own lives but themselves. The future doesn't always mean years from now or even months. It could be the very next second. It's all in the mindset.

One of my favorite film writers and producers, Ava DuVernay, once said, "Sometimes it only takes one yes to get you from where you are currently to where you have always wanted to be in life." I often wonder if everyone in this world gets that. Yes, you may have been waiting for a while, but when it happens, are you prepared? It's all about being and staying ready.

My family and friend would often call me "The Renaissance Man" or "The Man with the Plan." I always seem to know how to do something, or, I had a plan to get things done. Of course, I wasn't born with the knowledge; I had to first write out the plan, then research it to ensure that there were ways for me to achieve the plan. If I couldn't find a plan that worked best for me, I started from where I was, and used what I had, so I could execute the vision and continue to flourish.

It is sometimes hard for people to understand my thought process or my actions regarding my future. Maybe it is because no one has ever been in my shoes and felt the pain I felt when I was jailed in the foster care system or told that I wouldn't ever amount to anything based on my past and the history of my biological parents, especially my mother. However, I am an anomaly. It is not usual for one to feel burdened and still be able to reach any goal they put their minds to.

Conversing with my peers, I tell them to do the same thing that I have always told myself. "You cannot allow anyone to control your life because it will eventually take a toll on you." I've learned that you must have an open mind, have understanding, have the courage to sacrifice some things, and don't be so quick to talk but listen.

Success is not as easy as it is portrayed to be. Everyone's success will not be the same. When you look at Tiffany Haddish, her fame did not occur overnight. As a young African American, she experienced being in foster care while growing up, and struggled as a comedian while she tried to get in the doors to elevate her calling. She would spend countless nights being homeless and sleeping in her car until Kevin Hart loaned her a few dollars to help her get back on her feet. Now she is starring in movies and receiving countless awards.

Another example is Ralph Lauren. As a kid, his family couldn't afford new clothes, so he would receive his brothers' hand-me-downs. He didn't allow his predicament to stop him from going after what he believed in. He is now the namesake of one of the leading fashion brands in the world.

These success stories are examples to show you that you don't have to be raised with a silver spoon in your mouth to be your best self. No matter your circumstance, you will see the results once you speak to your situation and not about your situation. You've got to stop letting the dead parts of you speak to the living parts of you. Practice speaking well, even when you don't feel well.

ETHAN THE ANGEL

I thought I was finished writing this book. But had I not mentioned what you're about to read, you wouldn't be able to understand how important it is to be the friend that everyone needs at some point in their life.

About three weeks after starting my senior year at Bethune, the university called for a mandatory evacuation for all students who resided on campus. Hurricane Irma was on its way, and we had to leave by ten o'clock that evening. I didn't know what my next move would be because ten o'clock was fast approaching. A part of me wanted to get on a flight to the other side of the country, but the other part felt bad to leave my family and friends behind, especially since the hurricane was predicted to be extremely catastrophic and powerful. I rushed over to my residence hall to see that all the students were scrambling with their bags so they could evacuate. I figured they were from out west or up north, because all Floridians knew that we couldn't rely on weather forecasters one hundred percent. There had been past experiences where we were informed that we should evacuate, but the hurricane never came.

I went to my room and started packing, not knowing where I was going. Mama called and told me to come home, but I didn't think that was a smart idea since the entire state of Florida was under evacuation. One of my great friends, whom I'd met at college called me and started yelling at me, because I hadn't made plans to come to her house until we could go back to campus. She said something like, "Now you know there is space here for you. You have nowhere else to go, boy, so bring your ass on."

I could have gone home to be with my adoptive family, but that wasn't a drive I wanted to make. So, what did I do? I packed my items and went to her house. I didn't want to go over there because her boyfriend was staying there, and she was renting her second bedroom out to another friend of hers. I knew she really didn't like her boyfriend, but she had no choice but to deal with him because she'd let him move in and stay there.

When I arrived at the house, Mercedes and her boyfriend were arguing, so I tried my best to stay out of their way. That night I slept on the love sofa, as I always would any time I stayed over. Mercedes slept on the other sofa because she refused to sleep with her boyfriend. Waking up the next day, everyone in the house, except for me seemed mad at each other. I didn't know the reason, but I didn't let it phase me and went on my way and cooked breakfast. Mercedes continued laying on the sofa. She hadn't been feeling too well over the past month. No one knew what was wrong with he and neither did she. I wanted to encourage her to take a pregnancy test, but I knew that would have caused turmoil, especially since she and her boyfriend weren't getting along.

After breakfast, I turned on the television to watch the hurricane tracker, so we could decide on our next steps. I realized that we needed to get some items from the store just in case we lost power. On off the forecast, the hurricane would be a category 5 by the time it got on land. I told Mercedes to get dressed so we could get what we needed. Her roommate decided to flee up north, so that would be one less person we had to shop for. I made a list of what we needed, then we headed out.

Mercedes thought I was doing the most, but I wanted to be as prepared as possible. By the time we got to the nearest Walmart, most items on the list were sold out, so we worked with what we had. After

Walmart, we went to Dollar Tree to get some batteries. From previous experience, my family would remember to purchase everything else except for those, so we would have to carry a candle everywhere we went. Our last stop was to Chick-Fil-A to get some food. Once we got our food, we were on our way back to her house.

When we finally made it home, her boyfriend was on the love sofa eating a sandwich and watching a movie on Netflix. I couldn't finish my food because all I could hear was Mercedes in the bathroom, throwing up the Chick-Fil-A that we just had purchased. The situation aggravated my soul because no one knew what was going on with her, and her boyfriend would just sit there as if anything wasn't wrong.

A few days went by, and the hurricane had changed course. I was upset because we were all prepared, and I wanted to experience the hurricane that everyone was so afraid of. When it came to school, we had missed two full weeks of class because the University Emergency Management Office was convinced that the hurricane would hit, so they released us early from campus grounds.

The lights in the house eventually went off for about two days, but that wasn't long in comparison to other residents nearby. Mercedes would be lying down, sleeping, as her boyfriend continued to watch movies on his phone. I tried to feed her soup, but she would throw that up, too. I suggested she go to urgent care. I didn't think it was the best time because we were still feeling the aftereffects of the storm, but I was tired of seeing her suffer. After having a debate with her, we agreed to go to the Florida Memorial Hospital. Though Halifax Health Medical Center was down the road, I wasn't going to take her to that one. The wait time there was unbearable.

As soon as Mercedes signed into the hospital, they called her to be pre-screened. I went with her because I knew they were only check-ing her weight, temperature, and asking general questions before they made the decision on what they were going to do with her. After the pre-screening was over, we went back to the waiting room until they called her to the back. I decided to stay in the waiting room when she left the second time because I wasn't expecting a long wait time. Thirty minutes had passed, and I hadn't heard from or seen Mercedes. I tried texting and calling her, but the service in the hospital wasn't good, so I had to wait. I went to the check-in desk and inquired about her condition. I was told that she had been admitted and placed in a temporary room. It felt as if my chest had dropped to my stomach. I was afraid. I didn't know what the issue could be, but I knew I would soon find out because I was in-route to her room. When I got to her door, I put my ear up to it to see if I could hear anything, but there was only silence. I knocked on the door twice, and she told me to come in. When I saw her face red from tears and the pregnancy test on the counter, I knew she was pregnant. Though she was upset, she knew she had to woman up and do what was right. After calling her parents to tell them the news, and signing medical documents, she was discharged, and we were headed home.

Months went by, and her now ex-boyfriend had been asked to leave the house, and she was getting used to pregnancy life. She couldn't go through this pregnancy alone, and even though I didn't know much, I still did all I could for her. I went to all but two of her obstetrician-gynecologist (OBGYN) appointments, so the nurses and doctors believed that it was my baby, even though we'd always correct them; I was just glad I could be there to support her. I also stayed at her home just in case she needed assistance. Between her brother and I trying to support her every step of the way, she was spoiled. Whatever cravings she had, we either cooked or went to get it so we wouldn't hear her complain.

For about three weeks during her pregnancy, I left to complete a study abroad program in Senegal, West Africa. Though I was on the other side of the world, I still managed to communicate with her morning, afternoon, and evening. I was excited about going to West Africa, but I was even more excited about knowing the gender of the child, which we would find out when I returned to the States in about a week.

At the appointment, I informed the doctor that Mercedes couldn't know the gender until her gender reveal party. I knew I had to gather my thoughts and plan something quick, because everyone wanted to know what she was having, and no one knew except for me. We ended up having a gender reveal party at her job with her friends and co-workers. Also, I got on Facebook Live to record it so that her other family and friends could enjoy the moment as well. She was having a baby boy!

The last month leading up to the delivery, we had an OBGYN appointment every week at 9 a.m. Mercedes's brother had officially moved into the house with her, but he had an early class, so we all had to rush to her appointment. The wait time in the OBGYN was longer than expected, so by the time her doctor's appointment was over, I had to speed back so that her brother wouldn't miss class.

As we were driving toward the Main Street to the house, Mercedes turned on my gospel song, "Lord Do It," re-made by Bishop Hezekiah Walker. I was glad she turned it on because I liked listening to gospel music while driving, but I got into the song so much that I didn't realize I was speeding. I got pulled over on the side of the road by the county sheriff's department.

We were so nervous. I couldn't make an excuse for my excessive speeding. Mercedes told me to calm down and relax because everything would be okay. While we were waiting for the sheriff to get out of his truck, Mercedes got her vehicle registration and insurance papers, so we could hand them over to him once he asked. She then told me to get my driver's license out, so the sheriff wouldn't have to ask me to do so. I started sweating. I had my wallet, but I knew that I had lost my driver's license when I had visited California earlier in the year.

Yes, I know what you're thinking; why didn't you replace your license when you knew you had lost it? Well, if I could give you an excuse,

I'd say that I didn't like waiting for long periods of time, and every time I went by the Department of Motor and Vehicles (DMV), my wait time would be a minimum of thirty minutes. I talked myself into believing that I had time to replace my license since I had taken three defensive driving courses before getting my learner's permit. Mama didn't think I would understand how to drive unless she took me through many different driving courses.

When the sheriff finally got to my window and asked me if I knew why he'd pulled me over, I smirked, and told him, "Yes." He proceeded to ask for my license, vehicle registration, and insurance papers. I gave him everything except my license and informed him that I had recently lost it last week when I was in California. He returned to his truck and came back a second later to ask me for any type of identification, so he could check my record. I didn't have my passport on hand, but I did have a picture of it in my phone. (Thank you Shontericka for telling me to take a picture of it before leaving for our Winter Study Abroad program.) He called the dispatcher to tell them what had occurred with my license. The picture wasn't valid since it wasn't on hand, so then I was asked for my full name. I was hesitant in giving my full name because I knew that some of my legal documents had different last names.

I gave him six different names he could try: Jacari Harris, Jacari Williams Harris, Jacari Edward Williams, Jacari Etienne Harris, Jacari Edward Williams Harris, and Jacari Etienne Williams Harris.

After going through each name, I realized that none of them worked. The sheriff thought I was crazy, but I informed him that I was adopted, and my name had been confusing for quite some time now. I knew he didn't believe me when he rolled his eyes, but I didn't know what else to do. All I could do was apologize, then afterwards lie.

To speed up the process, I told him we were rushing back to the house to get papers for the OBGYN since she was about to have the baby; he believed me, too. He was working fast on his end; it was just my fault that we couldn't leave. I had nothing to show proof that my driving history was decent, and that was all he wanted to see.

As the picture of my passport information page didn't work, or my name, I gave him my own license plate number praying that it would work. It did not. The dispatcher believed I was lying, because according to their system there wasn't a car registered with that license plate number. I was confused since my vehicle was registered, and Mercedes was very concerned. Immediately, I was asked to state my social security number. After stating it aloud three times, the dispatcher informed the sheriff that nothing came up. I was worried. Why wasn't my information showing up in the system? I looked over at Mercedes, and I could feel the tears that were about to come down her face. She didn't know what was going to happen to me. I didn't know, either. Worst case, I would be going to jail.

Before I was let off without getting a ticket, the sheriff came back and told me, "Sir, according to our system, you don't exist. You really should look into that ASAP." I was startled. I didn't know if I was living a lie, or if I was who I thought I really was. What I did know was that the angels were watching over us because Gabriel was coming soon, and I didn't support her this long in the pregnancy to end up in a jail cell.

The next day, I started doing research and calling my adoptive and biological mothers to allow them to help guide me on what I should do to resolve issues surrounding my name.

BEING FOUND

When I realized my potential—that I am who I am because God used me for my mistakes—I began to spread my wings and soar. From living in an apartment with two bedrooms, one bathroom, and six brothers and sisters, to moving to multiple foster homes, to the house of the unknown that had four bedrooms and two bathrooms, to now living in a university residence hall. I realize I am here because I am a testament of how a little faith mixed with a little work can lead to one's life desires. Countless young lives are taken every year from issues that could have been avoided—whether from suicide, murder, or anything else. Those lives don't have the chances that you or I have today.

After seeing others my age struggle just to get by—just as I did mentally, emotionally, religiously, and financially—I realized I had to keep my sanity if I truly wanted the best for myself. Knowing how I can be an advocate for the speechless and a force to reckon with for the chained, I know that it's now time for me to step out and step up just a little more. The signs of no sleep have come. I will sleep when I have completed all the necessary tasks and have endured all that my strength will allow me to. I will be like the bullfrog who is alert even when one has the belief that he is asleep.

When I find that child out there—boy, girl, black, white, long hair, short hair, matted hair, no hair, no training, some training, no goals, no sense of self-worth, straight, gay, transgender, bi-sexual, queer, with trust issues, health problems, or mental health issues; when I find that family out there—big, small, perfect, un-perfect, successful, open-minded, selfless, willing, compassionate, caring, open arms...

When I find that strength out there that is mighty, strong, bold, courageous, powerful, determined, dedicated...

When I find that happiness that no man can take away from not a single soul...

When I can go into my home knowing that I have changed someone's life for the better—that is when I have become truly successful.

It will not be easy; I don't expect it to be. If anything comes easily, it can be easily taken away.

APPENDICES

Essential Tips for Fostering or Adopting

For those who may be interested in fostering or adopting a youth: Be open minded about what you are getting yourself into. Not every adoption is bad, and not every adoption is good. However, the way your mind is set when going into the adoption process will determine your success. If you are close-minded, expecting things to go a certain way, your adopted spirit that is supposed to be pleasant and welcoming will gradually change to sorrowful and regretful. Adoption is not just a simple signature of proclamation that you will keep the child under your custody. Adoption is growth. Growing pains will be your best friend in this process. Everyone has had a different walk in life; some make it, but others need special help that only you can offer to get them where they need to be in life.

Be understanding. When going through the steps of adoption, you must understand that the child wishes that he or she is not in the situation to begin with, or sometimes they really don't know what's going on; therefore, you must understand the importance of understanding a child's mindset and heart. Everything you wish to know about the child will not be given to you in black and white. Most things will come as days go by. You must understand that the child was not raised like you or, depending on their age, wasn't taught much. You must be that special someone who is willing to turn a negative into a positive so that he or she can see and understand the true meaning of happiness and love.

Sacrifice. One of the hardest things for anyone to do is give up something good to make something else work out. When adopting, your time, feelings, and money will be sacrificed. You will not be able to go and do as many things as you are accustomed to. Or, you may not be able to spend as much time with your significant other, because you are with your new adoptee. Sacrificing money will hurt you only if you let it. The investment will make you feel good in the long run. You will never be compensated enough for fostering or adopting any child. The check you receive from the Department of Children and Families will not compare to how much money you will have to put out on your own for your child to live a healthy, memorable, and joyous life. At the end of the day, collecting a check shouldn't be your goal. Sustaining one's life and being the best thing he or she ever had should be your concentration.

You should listen, not only with your ears but with your eyes, your heart, and your impacting touch. A lot of times, all a child wants you to do is listen. It may not make sense, it may not be right, but listen. Show the child that you care and that you will be there. The child doesn't know what it feels or looks like when someone is there for them. Remember, in most cases, it's not the child's fault that they are in the position they are in.

Lastly, you should believe. Believe that you can help a foster youth or adoptee in some way.

NAVIGATING THE SYSTEM OF FOSTER CARE AND ADOPTION

N o matter the circumstances, an adopted child will always have a clogged hole in their heart filled with nothing but unanswered questions, confusion, doubt, misunderstanding, and shame—a heart that yearns to be free from the issues and unwanted pain that is forced on them because they feel like they don't belong. Children are not property, and they shouldn't be treated as such. Children should be cherished, loved, respected, and protected.

Adoption in this day and time is most like the game of chess. There are so many decisions made for the innocent child, which can either give the child an advantage or disadvantage. These decisions, like living arrangements, history of biological family, information on their adoption, and so much more, can put a strain on a child's heart and mind, leaving them wondering if they truly matter or not to the people who tell them, "I love you." From infant to teenage adoptions, the child must deal with the affects then keep moving forward, no matter the challenges that arise.

There is a system in place that should be changed but won't be changed until the right individuals step up to the plate. This system gives the government authority to make decisions over a child's life, no matter who may have to face the consequences: the child, immediate family, or even the extended family. This system is the Department of Health and Human Services and Child Protection agencies. In the United States, adoption licensing requirements vary from state to state but are overseen by each state's Department of Child Protective Services or Human Services. Each state's services are monitored by the Department of Health and Human Services. Even though it is their responsibility to ensure the wellbeing of each child who enters the system, many decisions are made based on convenience, which doesn't take into consideration the future of the child's life.

I have come to realize that more money is spent on ensuring a child's superficial contentment in their new home than on creating effective programs that will benefit the biological parents so that they might be able to keep their child.

I believe in family preservation; however, in some circumstances, it is not an option. If there is no immediate or extended family members willing to take in the child after being removed from parents, then the child should be placed in care. Yet, what is needed to reduce the number of children in our world's welfare system are experts who can produce prevention programs for biological families, so the child won't have to be in the system in the first place.

There are people who believe that some parents aren't qualified to take care of a child. But to them I ask: Haven't you ever been told you weren't qualified or able to do something in life? Whether it was achieving a goal or overcoming an obstacle, you were given a chance to try until that very thing was accomplished. Sometimes, all people need is a push, resources, assistance, and maybe just a listening ear. But sometimes, by the time those things are received, it's too late.

We are living in a society where people know the issues of adoption but won't use them to ignite a positive change for our children, the future leaders of this world. The adoptee can face several issues with self-esteem, grief, separation, loss, and attachment. Adoption laws, policies, and practices differ from state to state and have not been consistent what a family truly is. Many families who start and go through the process of adoption lack access to pre- and post-adoption services. So many adopted people cannot even access their original birth certificates. I believe that having information of one's biological roots is a basic human right that impacts the mental, emotional, and developmental makeup of an adoptee.

Then we have those youth who age out of the foster care system without being adopted. Those age-out youth have no one to turn to because, when they are of legal age, they are kicked out into the real world to fend for their lives—especially if they don't have programs to assist them as a young adult. Furthermore, issues of race, class, and culture can make the challenges even more difficult for families and adopted individuals.

Every day we have children who enter a new home not knowing if that foster home will be their last stop. Many children are accustomed to moving from home to home over months, years. They come to expect it, sometimes not even knowing why. The welfare system believes that it knows exactly what the child is feeling, but how can it ever know unless the system itself was made up exclusively of those who had been in the same predicament themselves? And, even when the foster family who agrees to take in the child does their absolute best in functioning as a much-needed support system for the child, they will still never know the feeling the child has on the inside. Even if the youth is asked to explain how they feel—a question I was always asked—they can never really verbalize it, because, no matter the answer given, there are still so many other emotions at play too, constantly, relentlessly.

There are little boys who grow up doing drugs, drinking, fighting, dropping out of school and not having a plan for success in their adulthood, because their past circumstances have lingered on them for too long, because they were trapped by a system that thought it knew the formula for their lives but did not. There are little girls in foster care growing up abused, having post-traumatic stress disorder (PTSD), getting pregnant early, and not knowing how to love themselves, because they have been dropped off to different houses, hoping that the household family would want them to stay.

Once upon a time, I believed that the system was designed to fail vulnerable youth that are a part of it. But over years of being actively involved with foster care and adoption agencies, I see that while the system isn't designed to fail the vulnerable youth, it also doesn't maximize the opportunities for those same youth to live in peace in happiness.

Youth in the system are clothed and fed, at least most of the time, but many of them who I have met at conferences, camps, workshops, or at social events are missing the ingredients that makes a difference in human beings. They don't always feel that they're treasured or loved, and even if they have felt as if they are, most times they didn't trust that it was genuine. Instead, they grow up feeling they are unworthy of love. That breeds behavior that is sure to bring about emotional issues for their future.

That's why it is important to be up front and honest with a child. In my case, I only wanted to know the truth, because I felt as if I wasn't living the life that was meant for me. I was taken away from my biological family by the Department of Children and Families at a young age, and over time it became apparent that all facets of the process were not in the best interest of me as the child.

I've heard it said that, "Adoption was the best decision for you," but I, as the child, was not part of the decision-making process. My brother and I did not make any decisions about our next journey in life after being taken away from our family. We were too young. Peanut was three years old, and I was one. That gives the connotation that we wouldn't be able to comprehend the situation at the time to make the best decisions for our future lives, which is certainly true. Now that I am older and have a clear understanding of what occurred before I was born, before entering the system, and post-adoption I see now that many things should have been done differently that would have been in the best interest on not only myself, but for my biological mother and my other siblings who were taken away.

Some say, "God already had it planned for your life," but who's to say the process was approved by Him? We live by the choices we make, but when the choices are made by a stranger, the consequences are not paid by the stranger; they are paid by the child. That child will have to live a life with choices made my others, whether good or bad.

There are several types of adoption: adopting an infant in America, adopting a child from the American foster care system, adopting a child from another country, or even adopting a stepchild. Any child that fits in the category of having a legal guardian other than their natural parents is part of the adoption system and process, but that doesn't make them any less deserving of permanent, loving families of good character. I was adopted through the American foster care system, a system that takes in kids whose parents have first been reported for any of the following reasons: physical abuse, sexual abuse, neglect, incarceration, abandonment, truancy, or death to name a few. Some even voluntarily give up their children. I was placed in the system for neglect and parental drug abuse.

Once a situation has been reported to the child protection agency, in my case the Department of Children and Families, the agency that represents the child goes to court to seek temporary custody for the child. Once that is done, the case is assessed, and the case manager decides what should be done in the best interest of the child. If the child is taken away from his biological home and placed in foster care—a temporary living situation for children, whose parents cannot take care of them and whose need for care has come to the attention of a child welfare agency—then the agency does their best to find a foster home that is best suited for the child. The agency also tries to locate a family that is close in proximity to the child's original home to make the transition smoother for the child.

While the child is with the foster family, the agency works with the biological parent(s) to get them in a position where they can get their children back. My biological mother was given a case plan that informed her of what she needed to do to get us back. This case plan is usually created by the agency and the legal professionals overseeing the case. If the biological parent(s) doesn't adhere to the case plan, or if there are no other solutions to the issues at hand, the judge terminates their parental rights. Afterwards, a petition for adoption is filed. The process is long but worthwhile. Not everyone is meant to foster or adopt—but you will never know if you don't try. It is a leap of faith under any circumstances, but it can also change your life.

***

QUESTIONS TO CONSIDER

1. Can I be an asset in a child's life?
2. Do I want a child (biological or adopted) to live a better life than my own?
3. Can I sacrifice my wants to ensure that a child's needs are met?
4. Does my lifestyle allow me the time necessary to meet the needs of a child?
5. Do I have the patience to wait for an adopted or foster child to show me love?
6. Am I patient enough to complete the pre- and post-placement work?
7. Have I had a major life event in the past six months that would hinder me from being a good fit as a foster or adoptive parent?

If you answered "yes" to at least one of the questions, you have the chance to save a vulnerable youth in our foster care system who needs temporary care. Or, in some cases is eligible for adoption. However, if you didn't answer yes to at least one of the questions above, you still have time to help a child in some capacity. If not today, certainly tomorrow.

Spring is forthcoming.

Resources

Whether you want to connect with foster youth, adoptees, find information about financial and other types of available support or read legislation that is centered around foster care and adoption, here are some great places to start:

Families for All, Inc.

The certified 501(C)3 that I founded, Families for All's mission is to meet the diverse needs of children, birth parents, adopted individuals, adoptive families, and all those touched by adoption through advocacy, education, legislative action, and influence. Families for All is an impact, change and awareness public charity dedicated to finding loving families for foster youth and children who are eligible for adoption.

Learn more about Families for All: https://www.familiesfa.org/

First Star

First Star improves the lives of foster youth by partnering with child welfare agencies, universities, and school districts to ensure foster youth have the academic, life skills, and adult support needed to successfully transition to higher education and adulthood. Their mission is pursued through innovative college-preparatory programs, providing technical assistance to stakeholders, and advocating for policy change.

Learn more about First Star: https://www.firststar.org/learn-more/who-we-are/

Families First, Inc.

The first licensed adoption agency in the state of Georgia. Families First is committed to setting up youth for success by young adulthood by providing them with key services to overcome life's challenges and reach their goals.

Learn more about Families First, Inc.: https://www.familiesfirst.org/

Foster Care Alumni of America

A national nonprofit association that has been founded and led by alumni of the foster care system. FCAA provides opportunities for alumni to know each other, to share support and information, and to become an extended family for each other.

Learn more about Foster Alumni of America: https://fostercare-alumni.org/mission/

A Home Within

A Home Within is the only national organization dedicated solely to meeting the emotional needs of foster youth. They provide open-ended, individual psychotherapy, free of charge, to current and former foster youth.

Learn more about A Home Within: https://www.ahomewithin.org/

Creating a Family

Creating a Family is the national adoption & infertility education organization. Our mission is to strengthen families through unbiased education and support for infertility patients, adoptive parents, and allied professionals.

Learn more about Creating a Family: https://creatingafamily.org/about-us/

Child Welfare Information Gateway

Child Welfare Information Gateway promotes the safety, permanency, and well-being of children, youth, and families by connecting child welfare, adoption, and related professionals as well as the public to information, resources, and tools covering topics on child welfare, child abuse and neglect, out-of-home care, adoption, and more.

Learn more about Child Welfare Information Gateway: https://www.childwelfare.gov/

Dave Thomas Foundation

Through its signature program, Wendy's Wonderful Kids®, the Foundation provides grants to adoption agencies to hire recruiters who use an evidence-based, child-focused recruitment model to find loving, permanent homes for children waiting in foster care. The Foundation works closely with child welfare advocates and policymakers, provides free resources about foster care adoption and raises awareness through social media campaigns, public service announcements and events.

Learn more about The Dave Thomas Foundation: https://www.davethomasfoundation.org/

"It's my hope that I make each of you believe. Believe in what's good and right, believe in second chances, because in order to do that, you must believe that your story holds value. When you know who you are and whose you are, and you know your true and authentic identity, you no longer go around existing as something less than you really are."

-Jacari Harris

A Conversation with the Author

1. **How can the telling of your story affect your everyday life?**
   My upbringing was difficult, but my journey to finding my identity is never-ending. This book is my life. When people think of me, this first thing that they correlate me to is foster care and adoption. When they hear my name or learn my story and the strides that I am achieving each day to combat the issues faced by foster youth, adoptive youth, and those families affected, they too are propelled to find the very thing that they are passionate about and work toward making it better.

2. **Do you have additional thoughts that weren't part of the book?**
   When I first started writing, I was afraid to be transparent and vulnerable. However, my editors weren't having that—and that's why I love working with them. Latoya and Felice wanted the raw, uncut truth about my experience in foster care, in adoption, and in the achievement of my goals. At the end of the day, it is my story. There was no need to feel ashamed or afraid what others might say, because the truth of the matter is, we all have stories and we all should share them at some point in our lives. You can help someone else get through their situation by being open and sharing yours.

3. **Who do you love more—your biological parents or your adoptive parents?**

I love both my biological and adoptive parent(s) equally. I don't think it would be fair for me to love one more than the other, or to not love one at all. My biological mother, in my opinion, did one of the most amazing things that a human can do. She was able to build a new life in her body, or rather, God was able to build a new life through her. She had morning sickness, constant diet changes, and weight gain through the pregnancy term. I believe that bearing a child is an act of God. With that, she accepted that it required work, sacrifice, and a degree of suffering—and boy, she has told me many stories of how I was an aggressive kicker.

I started loving my father when I met him for the first time in the intensive care unit (ICU). Though I do not agree with meeting him in that setting, I am thankful that I had a chance to see and pray over him. When he passed away, I was angry with him for a few months because I would think day in and day out of how I did not get to experience my father like my other siblings and people in the community had.

My adoptive mother is like the frame to a puzzle in my life. Although she didn't give birth to me, she loved me like her own child, protected me, showed me the way, and raised me into the man that I am today. To know that her only daughter passed away before we arrived, and she still decided to take us in tells me that her love and strength is second to none.

4. **What have been some of the opportunities that have come your way since you began writing and speaking about your experiences?**

I have had the honor of inspiring many, especially foster and adopted individuals who thought they wouldn't amount to much since they were part of a system that they didn't get themselves into. I've encouraged others to be able to share their story, to be transparent, and to walk in their God-given purpose.

I never dreamed of visiting many cities like New York City, Charlotte, Los Angeles, Chicago, Orlando, Atlanta, and Washington, DC, or of speaking to large crowds about my story and how everyone can play a role in shaping a foster or adoptive youth life.

I never dreamed I'd be able to bring families together, help others find their biological parents, be the push that someone needs to move forward, or even be the "go-to" person for all things foster care and adoption. I never knew I had it in me.

5. **What is your current definition of success? How has your story affected your understanding of what it means to be successful?**
A successful person is one who can live and walk in their God-given purpose without doubt or fear! Success, I have learned through experience, comes with a great deal of discipline and understanding that you must give your all in everything that you do. When I first started speaking, I wasn't getting an honorarium or having my flight and hotel accommodated. I went at my own expense, knowing that one day I'd get a return on my investment. My message of hope mattered to people; it is what has got me this far and will take me all the way.

Don't get me wrong—I used to think I would never see the day that I would feel confident in myself or my identity. I didn't know who I was, where I came from, and how I came about until I decided to find the answers for myself.

6. **How did you go about getting the dockets 20 years after being in the foster care system?**

I first started writing in 2016. At that time, I had outlined each chapter in an old red notebook, but as weeks went on, I couldn't complete a sentence, and that is when I knew I really didn't know myself. I searched on Google to see if there were any resources and learned that I could retrieve court files from when everything took place. I contacted the Leon County Courthouse and started the journey to retrieve dockets. Each page of the file that I wanted was one dollar. Over time, I purchased all the pages as I knew that they'd give me a clear understanding of the process that my siblings and I went through.

I must admit, I was a bit nervous about retrieving the dockets. Imagine being two years old and hundreds of papers were submitted on your behalf from case managers, attorneys, judges, therapists, police officers, and others—and twenty years later you have a chance to read everything that happened to you from start to finish. I didn't know what to expect. I kept an open mind and was set free.

7. **What is the message you hope the reader will receive from reading this book?**

That you're worthy, you're special, you're powerful, and you're amazing. And it is my hope that everyone finds a role in shaping a foster or adopted youth life. "Adopt. If you can't adopt, foster. If you can't foster, sponsor. If you can't sponsor, volunteer. If you can't volunteer, donate. And if you can't donate, educate."

8. **If you had the opportunity to go back and do it all again, would this story be different? If so, how? If not, why?**

   No. I wouldn't accept the opportunity to go back and do it all again. My story made me the man that I am today. Because of it, I am stronger, wiser, and better.

9. **Every book has a legacy. What do you hope will be the long-lasting effect of the telling of your story?**

   It is my hope that the world will never look at foster youth, adoptees, and those who are affected by it the same way. That requires an understanding that everyone deserves an everlasting family. It is my hope that people will share their story—they too deserve to be listened to.

ACKNOWLEDGMENTS

B y far, this is one of the most challenging things I have ever done. I never thought I would be able to write a book such as this. Writing was never my niche; however, after spending countless years, months, weeks, and days up until the wee hours of the morning, I am glad that I have a finished a tool that will change the lives of many people around the world.

First, I must give honor to my Lord and Savior for instilling in me the desire to tell my story while educating many individuals on adoption. If it had not been for my adopted mother, Jessie Harris, my life would most likely be in shackles. Thank you for everything that you have done for me since I entered our home. Your kind words, never ending love, support, and wisdom has elevated me to a level that we both didn't know was in me. To my biological mother, Freddie McGee-Price, thank you for doing all that you can. Your support and love for me is endless. The best gift God has ever given me is seeing you overcome your substance abuse addiction.

While the writing and the memories are mine, there is no way I could have gotten through this journey without the help, support, and love from the following people:

- My cousin, Synthia Averhart, thank you for being my shield and always believing in me.

- My cousin, Shontericka Hall, thank you for being real with me the entire time and always reminding me that, "You gone be somebody special!"
- My go-to-person, LaDae Mathis, thank you for always checking on me.
- To my friends, whom I could look across the room and see you in the space reserved for Family: Christopher White, Andrea Cleveland, William Gomillion, Aminata Seye, Venesia Prendegast, Brian Brim Jr., Paige Graves, Gabriel Mason, Danielle Rodriguez, and David Rivers; it is an honor to know you, and I am thankful that you pushed me to complete my first book.
- My Olivia Pope, Ashanta Williamson, thank you for believing in me and reminding me that I have a purpose.
- To my Godson, Gabriel Williamson, you are in good hands.
- To Anya, Aaliyiah, and Aymin Gillette, your uncle loves you more than you could ever know.
- To my mentors, Adner Marcelin, Edward Tucker, Carneal Waddey, Cory Wright, and Leofric Thomas Jr., thank you for your wise words.
- To my life coaches, Attorney Benjamin Crump and Dr. Hakim Lucas; thank you for leading, guiding and supporting me.
- To my brothers and sisters, thank you for protecting me and guiding me.
- To my Spiritual Coaches, Cynthia Gaines and Ryan George; thank you for always lifting me up in prayer and reminding me that God has a divine plan for my life.
- To my church family, thank you for grooming me, raising me, and always showing your support.

- To my Bethune-Cookman University family, thank you for developing me into a leader, so that I can reach my full potential, and serve my community.
- To the Big Bend Community Based Care of Tallahassee, Florida, thank you for being with me through the separation and the adoption.
- My editors, Latoya Smith and Felice Laverne, thank you for bringing out the best in my first book and myself.
- To Monique D. Mensah, with Make Your Mark Publishing Solutions. Thank you for your assistance with the publishing process.

I would like to thank everyone who I have met throughout the chapters of my life. This book is for the overcomers, achievers and those who have the desire to want and do more to make our world better through our personal stories.

ABOUT THE AUTHOR

Jacari Harris, a native of Tallahassee, Florida, is an author, entrepreneur, life coach, business owner, and inspirational speaker. He entered the foster care system at an early age and was blessed to be adopted soon after. Jacari's story is proof that tragedies can position a person for a purposeful life. Jacari knows that tragedies will not define who he is or his goals. With the help of his loving adoptive mother and community, he defied the artificial limitations imposed upon him. He knows firsthand how to cope with adversity and overcoming hardship. His past has never held him back from accomplishing what he set his heart and mind to do.

After graduating high school, Jacari went on to complete an internship with national civil rights attorney Benjamin L. Crump, Esq. Thereafter, he earned his Bachelor of Science degree in Business Administration from Bethune-Cookman University and his MBA from Florida International University. While at Bethune-Cookman, Jacari was elected Student Body President and completed a study abroad in Senegal, West Africa. Interned with State of California Junior U.S. Senator Kamala Harris. He also is a 2020 recipient of Bethune-Cookman's 40 under 40 award, which recognizes the university's rising stars and influencers.

His devoted service to foster youth and adoptive individuals has led him to better serve the foster and adoptive community through his nonprofit organization, Families for All, Inc. This group offers advocacy for change, informing, connecting, and promoting the need for finding loving and committed families for fostering and/or adopting youth.

A sought-after speaker, Jacari shares a message of inspiration with the goal of helping others realize that they too can rise above the losses of life and be found anew.

SHARE YOUR STORIES

I would love to connect with you, and hear all of the ways this book has helped you become a better person, helped you realize your true potential, and all of the successful ways you find to apply my story of inspiration in your community and life. Please send me your stories. Nothing makes me delighted than to hear from you. When I get yours, I'll be sure to share it with the others who are waiting to hear stories like yours.

info@jacariharris.com